THE ESSENTIAL BEING

THE ESSENTIAL BEING
Psychoanalytic Understanding of Totalitarianism

Anamilagros Pérez-Morazzani
and Rafael E. López-Corvo

KARNAC

First published in 2017 by
Karnac Books Ltd
118 Finchley Road
London NW3 5HT

British Library Cataloguing in Publication Data

A C.I.P. for this book is available from the British Library

ISBN-13: 978-1-78220-500-5

Typeset by Medlar Publishing Solutions Pvt Ltd, India

www.karnacbooks.com

CONTENTS

ABOUT THE AUTHORS

Rafael E. López-Corvo, MD, is a medical doctor, psychiatrist, and psychoanalyst. He is a former associate professor at Ottawa and McGill Universities and Program Director of the Child and Adolescent Unit at the Douglas Hospital, McGill University in Montreal, Canada. He was also a member of the editorial board of the *International Journal of Psychoanalysis* for Latin America. He is a training and supervising psychoanalyst for the International Psychoanalytical Association (IPA), as well as the Canadian Psychoanalytic Society and the Venezuelan Psychoanalytic Association.

Anamilagros Pérez-Morazzani, PhD, is a psychologist and psychoanalyst from the International Psychoanalytical Association (IPA), the Latin American Psychoanalytic Federation (FEPAL), the Venezuelan Psychoanalytic Association, as well as a former guest member of the Canadian Psychoanalytic Society. She is also a former assistant professor of the Venezuelan Institute of Psychoanalysis.

PREFACE

In the introduction to his book *The Mind of Adolph Hitler*, psychoanalyst Walter Langer (1972) says the following:

> ... I like to believe if such a study of Hitler had been made years earlie. ... There might not have been a Munich; a similar study of Stalin might have produced a different Yalta; one of Castro might have prevented the Cuban situation. ... Studies of this type cannot solve our international problems ... They might, however, had led to the avoidance of some of the serious blunders we seem to have made because we were ignorant of the psychological factors involved and the nature of the leaders with whom we were negotiating. (p. 26)

There is a great amount of truth in this statement; one of the problems, however, is the fact that in general we find it easier to deal with concrete matters than to conceive abstract ones. It is always easier to see the obvious than to consider what is not so palpable. Until Copernicus, it was believed by astronomers that the earth was the centre of the universe (geocentrism) and not the sun (heliocentrism), because that was what was obvious. There are, however, other matters that interfere with the possibility of conceiving that traumatic facts, taking place during the first years of life, can have a decisive impact in our lifetime and always determine our own idiosyncrasy in later years. Mostly because these original traumas have been forgotten for being painful, but also because they have been structured according to the epistemology of childhood, we as adults no longer remember them. Besides, these early traumatic experiences are not really dramatic events easy to recall, but instead, they usually characterise imperceptible occasions cloaked by the banality of childhood, like "cumulative traumas", as Khan (1963) has described them. About the world of children, Girzone (1989) says the following:

> Children live in their own little world and to them it is serious business, and in their minds it all make sense ... but we can no longer enter into that world. It is lost for us forever. We were once there but somewhere along life's path have lost the key to that door that unlocks that world for us. (p. 5)

In this book we will try to compare the early years of the lives of two different groups of people: one group consisting of five well-known dictators and the other, used as a control group, representing an equal number of famous and creative individuals. The purpose is to establish how traumatic facts that we refer to as "pre-conceptual traumas", taking place during the early years of life, can determine the outcome of what any individual might do and how he or she will perform in the future. Pre-conceptual traumas are ubiquitous and determinant to all human beings of their own idiosyncrasy, of what they might become with time, what they would do, and even who they might marry; this represents a form of organiser that we could refer to, following Bion and Poincaré, as a "selected fact". What we have found, in matching these two different groups of individuals, is the similarity of the pre-conceptual traumas within each group, and the significant difference between each of them.

The crucial and most common finding present in the totalitarian group presents an older abused son, a violent father, poverty, paltry education, and young mothers in need of being rescued from the father's violence. In the other group, on the other hand, better education, financial conditions, and insignificant domestic violence were determinant.

We have chosen the term "essential being" to emphasise an important psychological quality present in all dictators, as a consequence of their unconscious narcissistic desire to conceive themselves as absolutely indispensable in order to fulfil their mothers' basic needs. Freud states that unconsciously some mothers can use their children, usually the boy, to fulfil their "narcissistic fault", meaning their phallic envy, induced by parental and cultural discrimination against them for being a woman, a need that can be enhanced in the face of a violent husband. We will examine these concepts further in Chapters One and Nine.

Children usually have to deal with many losses, such as weaning, parental separation, dilution of the mother's attention by the birth of another sibling, and so on. From a psychoanalytical point of view the emotions produced by such losses are referred to as "castration anxiety". Unconsciously, men and women deal basically with this anxiety using different means, women by having babies and men through competition; this is why women very seldom initiate war. In a family of three children, for instance, usually the elder is abandoned, the middle one forgotten, and the youngest abused, in the sense of parents stimulating dependency and attacking freedom in the young child, with the unconscious purpose of remaining parents forever.

Violence in the family is another important aspect to consider, often the consequence of the incapacity to distinguish between what is "alive" from what it is not; to be able to transmit to their children a sense of being alive, of being human, to feel that they deserve to be loved unconditionally, or, in other words, to feel loved for what they are and not for what they look like, do, or have. Previously in relation to these matters we have stated the following:

> But to be alive in the manner I am now advancing here, does not necessarily refer to the quality of being endowed with life, as it happens with animals or plants; it requires more precisely, a full awareness of being a "living human being" What then does it mean to be alive? It means the presence of an intuitive awareness of selfness, uniqueness, autonomy, continuous growth and, paradoxically, a sense of deadness. It requires a denotation of unconditionality, to feel loved for what you "are" and not for what you "have" or for what you "do". (López-Corvo, 2014, p. 10)

We have treated families where the common factor among all the adult members was the lack of awareness that they were alive, as self-contained and autonomous individuals; it was as if their lives did not belong to them and instead they were somebody else's project. They found it impossible to accept that introspection could be a better way to ease their mental pain than to privilege accumulation of material things. There was the unconscious feeling that they were like unborn foetuses depending on others and not being able to think for themselves and to take over their own lives; it was passively accepted by all and never questioned that the father was the only individual capable of exercising such a privilege, even though under close scrutiny he too was unable to do that.

This lack of awareness is something that can be observed in the complete disregard for life observed in suicide terrorists in relation to their victims as well as to themselves. We could summarise by saying that if the tiger were to be made aware of the gazelle's suffering it would starve to death! An unconscious feeling of "non-existence" will induce powerful feelings of envy towards anything sensed as being a "nice existence" or feelings of "well-being". In reference to this Bion (1970) says the following:

> "Non-existence" immediately becomes an object that is immensely hostile and filled with murderous envy towards the quality of function of "existence" wherever it is to be found. (pp. 19–21)

These feelings are personified by a "non-existent" person

> ... whose hatred and envy is such that "it" is determined to remove and destroy every scrap of "existence" from any object which might be considered to "have" any existence to remove. Such a non-existent object can be so terrifying that its "existence" is denied leaving only the "place where it was". (Bion, 1965, p. 111)

INTRODUCTION

Tyranny reveals a part of the soul that is usually awakened in sleep, when the rest of the soul—the reasonable, gentle and ruling part—is slumbering … Then the beastly and savage part, full of food and drink, casts off sleep and seeks to find a way to gratify itself. You know that there is nothing it will not dare to do at such time, free of all control by shame or reason. It does not shrink … It will commit any foul murder, and there is no food it refuses to eat. In a word, it omits no act of folly or shamelessness.

—Plato, *The Republic*

Tyranny is a habit capable of being developed, and at last becomes a disease.

—Dostoyevsky, *The House of the Dead*

Pre-conceptual traumas and "the butterfly effect"

It is quite amazing that when we compare the early years of the lives of different dictators, such as Hitler, Stalin, Mao, Hussein, and Castro, we find very similar circumstances, which are absolutely determinant in the structuring of their characters as well as their future behaviour. The evaluation and comparison of well-known creative individuals such as Freud, Picasso, Einstein, Gandhi, and Beethoven, on the other hand, also reveal very similar determinant conditions that have structured their personalities; however, such conditions, and future idiosyncrasies, are completely different from those observed in the group of dictators.

We have already referred to pre-conceptual traumas in previous publications (López-Corvo, 2012, 2013, 2014) as an experience all human beings go through in the first years of their lives, when a temporary absence changes into a permanent presence. Pre-conceptual traumas split the mind into two states—the "traumatised" and the "non-traumatised"—and will also determine the future personality of every individual, in a "butterfly effect". We will be describing these matters in detail in Chapter One.

The logic presented by the "butterfly effect" and the "preconceptual trauma" is structurally similar to what Freud revealed at the end of 1900 and the beginning of the twentieth century, that childhood events, considered as innocent and innocuous at the time, can have lasting and determining effects on the future behaviour of an individual. "Butterfly effect" refers to a sensitive dependence on small initial conditions that can produce variations in a distant future, in a domino effect. The concept represents a metaphorical exaggeration that states that the flapping of a butterfly's wings at a specific moment can, for instance, affect weather conditions in the future. We are using an analogous approach to the understanding of totalitarian behaviour, of how some events or pre-conceptual traumas occurring at an early age, determine an attitude in the mind of those individuals, which, when facilitated by certain environmental circumstances, can induce the emergence of a tyrannical ruler. It is the incidence of both dimensions continuously interacting, between men and the reality in which they have been immersed, that can induce specific traumatic events to become meaningful and operational.

In totalitarian systems, it is not just the "creed", the "doctrine", or the "socio-political" argumentation that in fact matters in the implantation of a tyranny; the true seed is the psychological profile of the dictator, his own narcissistic and private wants already determined by his pre-conceptual trauma, that induces him and his followers to remain in power forever and at any cost. The propaganda to sell "creeds" and "socio-political positions", which appears afterwards, carries the intention of deceiving and of concealing the true intention and main concerns of the dictator. For this type of leader, everything has to be at his service: people, money, as well as the well-known "cash box" used to buy the will of the people. The typical question from psychopathic coercion is: How do I make the other person's will bow down? By taking a position, by subsidising them, or with a threat? How do I divide? The dictator needs crisis in order to be recognised as the "saviour"; he has no role during peacetime. Societies led by these kinds of individuals live from crisis to crisis, always being continuously destabilised.

This is why we can find in the history of all totalitarians regimes—from left as well as right, communists as well as capitalists—exactly the same despotic way of ruling and the same criminal idiosyncrasies, where the only belief is that "the end justifies the means". Take, for instance, Hitler and Stalin, who were not only contemporaries but bitter enemies, embracing contradictory political doctrines, and who fought to the death during the Second World War. In a private conversation in June 1933 (Rauschning, 1940), shortly after being appointed Germany's Chancellor, Hitler had this to say about the Civil War in the United States:

> Since the Civil War, in which the Southern States were conquered, against all historical logic and sound sense, the Americans have been in a condition of political and popular decay ... America has ever since been drawn deeper into the mire of progressive self-destruction ... The beginning of a great new social order based on the principle of slavery and inequality were destroyed by that war, and with them also the embryo of a future truly great America that would not have been ruled by a corrupt cast of tradesmen, but by real *Herren*-class that would have swept away all the falsities of liberty and equality. (pp. 68–69)

Fortunately for future generations, it was him, and the gang of murderers who infiltrated the Nazi party, who proved to be "progressively self-destructive". We can compare this statement with what Marx had to say in the *The Communist Manifesto*, the theoretical quintessence of the Bolshevik revolution:

> Hitherto, every form of society has been based, as we have already seen, on the antagonism of oppressing and oppressed classes. ... The modern labourer ... instead of rising with the process of industry

sinks deeper and deeper below the conditions of existence of his own class. He becomes a pauper, and pauperism develops more rapidly than population and wealth. And here it becomes evident that the bourgeoisie is unfit any longer to be the ruling class in society, and to impose its conditions of existence upon society as an overriding law. It is unfit to rule because it is incompetent to assure an existence to its slave within his slavery, because it cannot help letting him sink into such a state, that it has to feed him, instead of being fed by him. Society can no longer live under this bourgeoisie, in other words, its existence is no longer compatible with society. (Marx, 1848, p. 93)

In a letter written in October 1861 on the same subject of the American Civil War, Marx stated:

The whole movement was and is based, as one sees, on the *slave question*. Not in the sense of whether the slaves within the existing slave states should be emancipated outright or not, but whether the twenty million free men of the North should submit any longer to an oligarchy of three hundred thousand slaveholders …

And further on:

The present struggle between the South and North is, therefore, nothing but a struggle between two social systems, the system of slavery, and the system of free labour. The struggle has broken out because the two systems can no longer live peacefully side by side on the North American continent. It can only be ended by the victory of one system or the other. (Marx, 1861)

The messages expressed in each of these two quotations are completely contradictory; however, both dictators, Stalin and Hitler, justified their criminal destruction of fellow men with propaganda that paradoxically portrayed how much they cared about them whilst always trying to conceal the true intention of keeping themselves in power. The true and sole desire of all dictators is to remain in power at any cost and regardless of any consequences; any other actions are absolute forms of concealing the intention to preserve control indefinitely and further the illusion of an "indispensable being".

When we examine the early years of life of Stalin, Mao, and Hitler, we find that they were opposite in their political beliefs but uncannily similar in terms of the traumatic events that surrounded the first years of life. All came from poor households; each had dead siblings prior to their births, becoming then the older child; they grew up exposed to extreme violence; their mothers were young women married to violent, despotic, alcoholic, and absent fathers, and were also direct targets of their brutality; their mothers felt extremely attached to these particular sons, overprotecting them to the extreme, not only because they felt afraid to lose them but also because they considered them their saviours. The particular aspects of childhood trauma in the lives of the five tyrants who are considered in this essay will be reflected in more detail in Chapter Two.

The case of Moses

Since we did have had the opportunity of personally interviewing any of the dictators or the creative individuals, we thought that perhaps the investigation of a patient who presented with similar characteristics to those found in totalitarian leaders could be beneficial. Moses was a forty-four-year-old man we had the opportunity to treat some time ago, when he was admitted to a therapeutic community due to chronic abuse of cocaine. The main characteristic of his pathology at that time was a cyclothymic oscillation of affects, sometimes up and sometimes down, although more frequently down. Recurrent depressive states with meaningful suicidal ruminations induced in him two forms of defence: the use of cocaine, and counterphobic mechanisms to the extent of him becoming a skydiver.

A few months after his admission, Moses became a natural leader in the community; however, instead of using this capacity in favour of a better integration of the group, his concealed purpose was to split the community into two opposing groups: the patients and the therapists. A more careful investigation revealed the existence of a similar repetitive pattern present in previous situations, such as workplaces, from which he was always fired when attempting to split the organisation by generating conflict between employees and management. At seventeen Moses was part of a leftist guerrilla group—having participated in several bloody encounters with the army—that he was forced to abandon due to health complications.

He was the older of four siblings, three boys and a girl. Shortly after his second brother was born, he went to live with his maternal grandparents: "I was some kind of a gift," said Moses. He grew up spoiled to the extreme by his grandparents who he financially helped by selling sweets that were made by his grandmother in the streets of the same town where his parents and sibling were also living, although in much better social conditions. He grew up with extreme resentment about this unfairness, a difference that was difficult for him to understand even after he had grown up. There was a fantasy that his father doubted his paternity because Moses looked very different physically from his siblings: "darker skin, kinky hair, and thick lips".

Moses grew up with deep feelings of injustice, rage, and impotence, harbouring revenge against anybody that had financial or social power over him. There was deep pain in the face of any sense of exclusion, which in time turned into easy "hatred of the rich", as he frequently expressed it. One day he confessed: "I never understood why my parents sent me to live with my grandparents away from my own siblings." Moses' grandmother, a tough and illiterate woman, strongly influenced Moses, structuring his character and way of being; even his name was chosen by her, possibly indicating her need of a saviour. She also sheltered long-standing feelings of anger and envy against her own daughter—Moses' mother—due to financial discrepancies as well as to feelings of shame and contempt. Progressively, Moses became his grandmother's agent of revenge against his own parents, being continuously pampered and applauded with enthusiasm for any individual achievement or excess. Moses, of limited intelligence and of concrete thinking, has, as an adult, to continue to search, in others, for the same pampering and applause he once obtained as a child from his grandmother. He had deep feelings of helplessness, anger, and destructive envy towards any situation he could not control, while, at the same time, he looked for applause and flattery from those he had convinced into following him.

The history

History has often witnessed the establishment of dictatorial systems: from the right, in early ages, and from the left, after the French Revolution, although more categorically, after the Russian Bolshevik uprising, when, influenced by Marx and Engels, social rights were instituted at the beginning of the twentieth century, or as Chomsky (1989) states:

> The Bolshevik revolution gave concrete expression to the Leninist conception of the radical intelligentsia as the vanguard of social progress, exploiting popular struggles to gain state power and to impose the rule of the "Red bureaucracy" ... (p. 45)

Countries in the northern hemisphere, such as Sweden, Norway, England, or Canada, have taken a socialist trend, where, alongside a trustworthy legal structure supporting human rights and conscious awareness about communal needs, there is also the strong presence of a capitalistic spirit, where money is privileged over humanity. But, regardless of these small flaws, these countries strongly and legally reinforce democratic means, always favouring communal and legal powers over any personal interest. Dictatorships on the other hand, communist as well as capitalist, are more often seen on other continents such as Europe, Asia, Africa, and Latin-America, perhaps as a corollary to some particular social dynamics present in these cultures. Russia, for instance, has never experienced a political system based on total freedom; first the monarchy, whose Tsars were addressed by common people as "little mother" and "little father"; then the totalitarian regime of communism; until very recently, liberated by Gorbachev, facing again the threat of power-hungry Vladimir Putin.

The pioneers who came in the 1500–1600s to colonise North America arrived with their own families and did not mix with local tribes, remaining, until now, culturally and ethnically different from them. The Spaniards, who came to conquer and Christianise the southern hemisphere, were mostly single; many were ex-convicts released for this purpose. They cohabitated and blended with local Indians, generating a mixed breed of illegitimate children. Up to the present, within lower socio-economic strata in Latin countries, there are single mothers who have given birth to several children each from a different father. Because illegitimacy is experienced as something dishonourable, it is customary for individuals always to expose their legitimacy, in order to protect themselves from such a shame, by signing with two surnames, the father's first and the mother's last; as opposed to illegitimate persons who would have to use only their mother's name. Such an irresponsible form of absent paternity carries numerous consequences, including the envy of illegitimate individuals towards legitimacy[1], as well as ambivalent feelings towards aggressive father figures. There are other issues, such as, for instance, machismo, invented by mothers who need to prove that their son's sexuality is absolutely indisputable, either sexually by making women pregnant, or aggressively by bullying other boys. Girls, on the other hand, are often restrained by their families, with the purpose of controlling their sexuality by inducing guilt and making them more dependent than boys.

Dictatorship is a form of government frequently found in Latin American countries, something that could have its roots in these sociological matters. Politically, illegitimacy is reflected in the attitude of a segment of the population towards leaders, preferring the aggressive and possessive over the more passive. Dictators are seen as representing the strong and overprotective father figure that has never been had, while the democratic leader, respectful of the law and capable of surrendering his tenure at the end of his term, is perceived as weak and absent, as their true fathers were in the past. An unconscious symbiotic link is then established between the leader and his followers, where they both incessantly nurture each other's needs, the follower rewarding his call for a present and powerful father, and the dictator fulfilling his rapacious need for unlimited power.

What then is behind this unrestricted desire to exercise power over others, disregarding any human concern? All totalitarian leaders portray the following emotional characteristics: narcissism, extreme envy, paranoia, perversion, and a strong need for revenge. Narcissism is present in the sense of being extremely self-centred, controlling, omnipotent, inclined to bouts of narcissistic rage if frustrated and in need of continuous adulation of personality. Such feelings constitute defences that were fostered in order to deal with related features present during their upbringing. We will examine these issues in the Chapter Two, devoted to the dictators' early traumas.

Two different groups of individuals

We will attempt to compare the effects that early traumatic experiences, which we refer to as "preconceptual traumas" have over two different populations of individuals. On one hand, there are characters well-known in political history because of their responsibility in creating and sustaining totalitarian regimes. On the other hand, there is the group of individuals known for their outstanding creativity in different fields. In the first group, or group A, we have chosen Lenin, Stalin, Hitler, Mao, Castro, and Hussein. In group B we have investigated personalities such as Beethoven, Freud, Gandhi, Einstein, and Picasso. However, before we venture into a comparison of these two groups, we would like to consider what we have referred to as "preconceptual traumas".

Obviously, the material we have used to establish the comparison between the two groups is a second revision—an analysis based on what others have said about the early lives of these individuals; it is not the front line information we gather during a psychoanalytic therapy, so we have relied on what biographies have already informed us of. Finally, the choice of the individuals discussed in both groups was made according to the amount of information we were able to gather, mostly from reliable biographical studies that have already been published.

CHAPTER ONE

Pre-conceptual traumas as a determinant factor in the individual's personality

The now that passes produces time, the now that remains produces eternity.

—Boethius, *The Consolation of Philosophy*

Pre-conceptual traumas, diachronically structured as a narrative of conjoined presences of absences, stand for highly toxic and emotionally organised 'parasites' that inhabit the unconscious mind from very early, feed on time and space, inhibit processes of symbolisation, are projected everywhere and reproduce themselves incessantly, thereby determining not only all forms of psychopathology, but also the idiosyncrasy of every existing individual.

—López-Corvo, *Traumatised and Non-traumatised States of the Personality*

Pre-conceptual traumas

We have defined "pre-conceptual traumas" (López-Corvo, 2014) as those events that take place during the early years of life of all individuals. They are the consequence of two main factors: first, the discrepancy between the supremacy of the parents and the helplessness of the child; and second, the fact that parents are just ordinary people, never chosen by God, as children's idealisation usually induces them to believe. Pre-conceptual traumas take place whenever a temporary presence or fact changes into permanent absence. The change of any transitory incident into a lasting and chronic one hinges on an imaginary equation, between the particular impact of the traumatic experience and the capacity of the environment to contain such an event and turn it into something harmless and meaningless.

Imagine, for instance, a thirsty, two-legged dinosaur, perhaps a tyrannosaurus that walked slowly to the edge of a lake that has now disappeared, in order to quench its thirst. One hundred and eighty million years later heavy showers uncover footprints engraved in the limestone revealing the footsteps of that thirsty dinosaur's early walk. It might have been a regular uneventful act, repeated every day, except that this time the existence of a series of variables conjoined to preserve the footsteps. Perhaps the massive weight of the animal together with weather conditions—such as temperature, humidity, the quality of the sand, and so on—managed to preserve the tracks forever. It means, in summary, that now, when there is no longer a lake and the dinosaur has been erased from the face of the earth, its footprints, produced in just one instant, have become preserved for eternity; or, in other words, what should have otherwise been a temporary event became a permanent one; an overwhelming absence became a significant presence. It might sound like a form of reductionism when we say that all human beings have dealt, and are and will be dealing, unconsciously, with some form of childhood trauma; however, a simple empirical psychological observation will allow any keen eye to come to terms with this statement.

Sometimes pre-conceptual traumas can be rather easy to follow; other instances, however, can be so diluted that it becomes difficult to put them together. Masud Kahn (1963), a British psychoanalyst, once referred to this form of injury as "cumulative trauma". A clinical vignette could be useful: a young girl appeared very disturbed, presenting a paranoid delusional system where she felt threatened by obscure forces that were accusing her of being a lesbian. She was the daughter of two pleasant and conscientious paediatricians, and, in spite of a thorough investigation, we could not find any childhood event capable of explaining the intensity of her mental suffering; except for the fact that she was the eighth child of a family of ten children. By the time she was born, her mother was "eight times diluted", and this "passive absence" of a mother's necessary presence was at the heart of her need and her paranoid delusion. It was an everyday, apparently attenuated, trauma, which had otherwise produced, in time, a vast and determining effect on her mind.

Usually traumas can be understood within a few hours of interview. In private practice, it is essential to determine, as soon as possible, the specific characteristics of the particular trauma that patients have experienced in early childhood. Some of these true characteristics can be inferred from the manner in which patients communicate their emotions to the therapists—something Freud referred to as the "transference", or how the patients *transfer* to the analyst those specific emotions—and also how the therapist responds emotionally to those feelings projected by the patient—something Freud referred to as "counter-transference". As stated earlier, these emotions have previously been experienced towards parents or other persons present during infancy, related to traumatic conditions that have remained frozen inside the unconscious mind.

Two types of traumas

We have formerly considered (López-Corvo, 2013, 2014) the existence of two different forms of trauma, as follows: one *universal*, referred to as "pre-conceptual trauma", which is present in all human beings. It takes place during the first years of life, when there is not a mind capable of providing the traumatic facts with a meaning; another, *accidental*, considered as "conceptual trauma", taking place at a time when there is already a mind, which fails to contain an overwhelming traumatic reality. By means of a failure in reality testing, there is always a continuous emotional entanglement between conceptual and pre-conceptual traumas. Pre-conceptual traumas split the mind into two opposite states that continuously interact: "the traumatised and the non-traumatised". The "traumatised state" is a direct consequence of pre-conceptual trauma that transforms with time as it repeats compulsively and continuously. The "non-traumatised state", on the other hand, represents the mental development that will normally take place from birth to adulthood.

Another significant aspect of childhood trauma is the difficulty in remembering its emotional aspect; it can be recalled intellectually, but the related emotions usually remain repressed. A young woman asked about her three-year-old boy who started the unpleasant habit of spitting everywhere and at everybody. I asked if she wanted this behaviour to disappear or to remain forever; she immediately answered, "Of course, to disappear". I said: "Well, then say nothing, it will eventually extinguish itself, but if you get into a continuous struggle with him he might stubbornly stick to his demeanour for a very long time." A year into his analysis, a patient brought a dream where he awakes in terror, feeling that he is choking because he cannot swallow something. He said he remembers having this dream several times before. He does not recall any event from the previous day that could have triggered this dream, although he remembers he was dealing at work with a very difficult problem that was demanding a lot from him. I said, "You mean that perhaps this problem is choking you?" "Well," he answered, "sometimes I feel I worry too much, that I could get fired and my family will suffer, although I know at the same time that it would be impossible to be laid off because of something like that." I asked if there was any situation in his childhood when he felt like choking. "Yes," he said. "When I was around four or five years old, I was visiting my maternal grandmother and then swallowed several aspirins from a bottle and was brought to the hospital where my stomach was pumped; it might have been something extremely unpleasant." I asked if his family was there, and he said that all of them were there, his mother and dad and his grandmother, and that he learned from his mother afterwards that the next day his grandmother had a stroke, was taken to the same hospital, and eventually died. He does not remember, but the fact that she could have died because of what he did could have made him extremely guilty. Then I said: "Now we know what choked you!"

Childhood represents the most vulnerable time in the lifespan of any human being, when certain conditions manage to break through the "protective shield" that nature has provided us with, and can no longer be contained, assimilated, or digested by the mother's enthusiasm to protect her baby, and for some particular reason change a temporary event into a permanent issue, which will eventually become a "time trap". The order of birth, the gender, the psychological characteristics of the parents, genetic disorders, accidents, diseases, and so on, can become traumatic. They will become "footprints" or dimensions that will eternally haunt the mind, reproducing immediate behaviour, ways of acting, without us being at all aware of them. The mind "alive", or *élan vital*, to quote Bergson (1911), performs differently from a dinosaur's "inanimate" footsteps; it provides "life" or emotions to the footprints, similar to the mind that invents a ghost to compensate for a lost limb, or the choking sensation of our previous patient. These conditions represent the "traumatised state of the personality", events, driven by chance, that can be so protean, of such infinitude of forms, that they become completely personal, just like our fingerprints. It is similar to the concept of "constant conjunction", originally introduced by the philosopher David Hume and later borrowed by Bion (1967) "to explain how a fact points to another, although the ideas implicit in both are not at all related" (López-Corvo, 2003), where facts that were conjoined by chance will remain associated forever.

"Projection" seems to be the most common psychic defence found in children against early traumas; in other words, the need to place outside, into the external world, fundamental aspects of the trauma. This mechanism of defence will be extensively maintained through the individual's life, to the point that it will be continuously repeated without the person involved having any awareness of it. Let us see some examples.

A patient was systematically abused by a psychotic mother who, every day after school, for as long as she could remember, forced her to continuously listen to whatever nonsense she could think of. "It was like a radio you couldn't turn off." She tried to escape from such a "torture" by wandering in her mind, whilst looking at the clock and desperately wishing for time to move on quickly. This mental wandering in order to escape, whilst at the same time giving the impression of being very attentive to her mother's chitchat, developed later into a sort of hyper-critical attitude, of being very attentive but at the same time very critical and disapproving of what other people might be saying to her. "It was," I said, "as if it were impossible for you to get rid of your mother because now your mother is everywhere." She produced a dream where she was in a boutique trying to buy a dress, but found to her surprise that in the shop there was only one type. They were on a very large rack and all had exactly the same design. Later she associated the dress pattern with one her mother once purchased for her when she was a little girl. "You are right," she said. "It is as if my mother is everywhere, like the dresses were in the shop." Another patient who suffered from phobic attacks, and who had been operated on as a child due to spina bifida—a genetic disturbance of the lower spine—once had a dream of a very large city with only one street going up and down—like San Francisco.

She associated the street with her spine as if her operation was also all over the place.

Analogous to a wheel running on a track, reality touches only one point, rests on one instant, the present, while incessantly flowing from the past to the future at the pace of Heraclitus' river.[1] If reality represents a temporary event circumscribed to one instant, we can then ask: What set of circumstances, like those that granted eternity to the dinosaur's footprints, might have sufficient weight as to change what otherwise would have been a person's transient moment into something permanent? What would make a temporary absence a permanent presence? Or, even more: How do these particular traumas determine an individual's future demeanour, his way of living or acting?

We have previously referred to the case of Elena (López-Corvo, 2006b), a thirty-four-year-old schoolteacher, who was dealing in analysis with the mental pain induced by her parents' divorce when she was only three years of age. In the transference, it was obvious that her fear of trusting, as well as her need to control, was possibly a defence against her apprehension of being rejected, forgotten, or ignored. She always took off her shoes before she lay down on the couch. This time she was wearing boots, but did not take them off, as she usually did; this was something I noticed but did not remark on. She mentioned an argument with her father, and realised that she seemed to harbour much resentment. She had a dream: there was a huge cockroach and she killed it, but then out of it came something like a thousand small ones. She referred to a classmate who was rather contradictory, could say terrible things, and then would say the opposite. The other day this friend said that Elena's feet smelled, and then, when Elena stood up to put a book on a shelf, she said that Elena had a "tight ass", that she could "crack all the books with her ass". I said that I was wondering if her fear of being dirty makes her not want to take off her boots. She denied it and said that she did not because it was too much trouble; I did not believe what she said, but said nothing. Then I said that feet, if dirty, could be washed, that it is something temporary. However, if the dirtiness comes from her "tight ass", it is permanent and it could be related to the feeling that her father abandoned her because she had a dirty ass that attacked and destroyed him. In this case, it would become a permanent issue, like the cockroach that multiplied into a thousand, because it was impossible to get rid of it.

External reality, because it is continuously becoming, is usually temporary; you can often avoid external reality, but inner threats are always present. Splitting space changes a fact from private to public; splitting time changes a fact from temporary to permanent, as in the transference. Dinosaur footprints have been there for many years, meaning nothing to the neophyte eye, but meaningful in the mind of a geologist. There are un-thought thoughts that pressure the mind until they produce an apparatus for thinking that demands containment and understanding. Traumatic thoughts are un-thought thoughts that endlessly repeat themselves searching for an answer, like a mind that invents a ghost limb to compensate for a lost one.

Let us examine another case. Kelly started the session by saying that she had lowered her status in her new job, in comparison with the previous one. "In my new job I am a designer while in the previous I was an art director." However, she feels better in her new position because "people are nicer". I said that she has doubts about her true self because she feels that she needs others to certify her status. After a pause she states: "There is something very important I want to tell you. My mother insists that I am bulimic, that she heard me vomiting in the bathroom and that is absolutely false and I denied it but she insisted and told my father who believed her, although I insistently told him it wasn't true. I am concerned because she will make me do something." She looks worried. I asked: "What does that mean, do something?" "Well, to see someone I guess," she answered. "Like whom?" "A doctor, I guess." I then said that she seems to be dealing with much confusion at the same time; that she is convinced, and is also trying to convince me, that she will be unable to produce a sensible argument for her mother about the vomiting, and, even worse, she will not be able to convince the doctor either, who will be, like her father, an extension of her powerful and dangerous mother; that I was wondering if she might be dealing with something else. "Well," she answered, "my mother could kick me out of the house like she did with my brother." She remained silent for a while and then said that she remembered a scene where she is at the hospital, in a tall bathtub—or maybe it is she who is little, perhaps five or six years old—and her mother is washing her hair, or giving her a bath: "I had a feeling then and now, that I touched the bottom, a feeling of emptiness and hopelessness. I think it might have been before or after the operation." I then said to her: "I wonder if it could have been before the operation, that she was bathing you for the operation, when you asked her if you could go home with her, if she was taking you with her afterwards and she said no, that you had to stay for the operation the next day, and then you felt hopeless, as if that was it, that you had touched bottom, like someone condemned to capital punishment who had extinguished all resources of pardon. The problem for her seems to be the tremendous power she feels her mother still has over her, which might come from that experience, as if she has jumped back in her mind nineteen years, as if time has not elapsed since, as if she is still five or six years old and can do nothing about it, feeling, as she felt then, like a helpless little girl.

How to catch a monkey and the "protean" falsifications of early traumas

The issue of traumas being projected everywhere reminds me of three matters: one is Nicholas de Cusa's definition of God as "a circle whose circumference is everywhere and whose centre is nowhere"; the second and third are evocative of two other issues, one referring to how local people in India catch monkeys, the other I associate with Proteus, a god created by the fertile mind of Homer.

Indians secure an empty coconut shell to a tree trunk and open a small hole big enough to place a nut inside. Once the monkeys are aware of the nut, they place their hand inside and seize it, but since their fist is bigger than the hole, it becomes impossible to pull the hand out of the coconut shell. The monkeys obstinately clutch the nut and never let go, allowing them to be easily captured. Perhaps we could say that in this case "the nut gets hold of the monkey". Similarly, the mind seems to clutch emotional tribulations present in early traumas with such a fury and intensity that they trap the individual in a continuous "repetition compulsion"; the emotional idiosyncrasies of early traumas mirror the stupid stubbornness of the monkeys.

The fact that Homer opted for Proteus to be a god from the sea—also named the "Old Man of the Sea"—associates Proteus to a mother's issues (Latin: mother = *mater*, sea = *mare*; French: mother = mère, sea = mer); also very much related to our topic, "Proteus" comes from the Greek word *protos*, meaning "primary importance", from which the word "protean" is derived. The god was not only capable of foreseeing the future but, most importantly, he had the faculty to change his external form or appearance into anything he wished. He could answer questions about divination only if he was pinned down and immobilised. In the *Odyssey* (Book IV), in the mouth of Menelaus, Homer describes the encounter with the god Proteus:

> As you know [said Menelaus], I was held down for seven long years in Egypt. And when at last the gods relented and sent a homeward breeze, I only made it as far as an island off the mouth of the Nile before I was becalmed. A goddess took pity on me as I paced the beach in desperation. "My father is the Old Man of the Sea," she said. "You and three picked men of your crew must catch him and pin him down." She helped us with disguises, the hides of seals which stank to high heaven. She even rubbed ambrosia under our noses against the stench. And when the Ancient came for his midday nap amongst the seals, as was his custom, we jumped him and held on for dear life. He had an awesome power, you see, to change his form—to lion, to snake, to boar, to gushing fountain and towering tree. But when he saw that we weren't about to let go, he reverted to his original shape and began to speak.

This is exactly what happens when we manage to help patients "pin down" their early pre-conceptual trauma, once the trauma is recognised in spite of any shape it might take. Only when we manage to recognise the particular trauma will the trauma "begin to speak". Let me refer to a case. At a point in the therapy of a couple, the wife refers to a dream. She is in town A and wishes to go to town X, but her husband is not there and nobody else seems to be able to help her, so she decides to go by herself. She walks for two days through a forest and then starts to climb a steep hill. She fears falling down and wakes up. When asked what was in town X that she wanted to reach so emphatically, she answered that in this particular town she gave birth to her only child. I said that it seems as if she wishes to have another child. She answered that it was impossible, because her husband, after her only child was born, decided to have a vasectomy. Later on it became clear that her husband was often bullied by other classmates when he was in primary school, because he was rather short in stature and, being the son of Middle Eastern immigrants, he had language difficulties and the children made fun of him for that as well. When he was three years old his sister was born, and later came to represent the part of himself that was smaller and unable to speak properly. When he returned from school, usually angry and frustrated, he became very abusive to his sister, and in reaction his father became physically very abusive to him. He felt he could never win. Later on, when he got married, he felt in control and by refusing to have children he felt capable of doing what he so much wanted to do but was unable to: to get rid of his sister by denying her birth.

The hypothesis sustained in this essay is that some personal traumas containing certain specific characteristics, together with a number of facilitating social circumstances, can place an individual in a certain position where he can gather power that will eventually, with time, develop into a tyranny. In the next chapter we will be considering some of these traumas.

Cain's mark

Cain was the elder son who dedicated himself to cultivating the land, while Abel looked after the flock of sheep. The Lord, suspiciously tainted with human unfairness, privileged Abel's offerings over those of Cain, inducing jealousy and envy that eventually led to murder. If we know something about sibling rivalry, we can conjecture that the envy, which was already there from the very beginning, from the older Cain toward the younger Abel, had set up a predisposition that exploded under the effect of the Lord's inequitable way of dealing with each of them. God then set a punishment Cain considered too unforgiving, and Cain feared that he would be recognised by someone and put to death. The Lord responded by setting a "protective" mark that would allow others to recognise Cain so as not to harm him.

We could interpret "Cain's mark" as the precise configuration made by the pre-conceptual trauma in the mind of each individual, leaving a "mark", a "selected fact"[2] that organises the personality and deter-mines significant aspects of the idiosyncrasy and identity of all human beings. These traumas represent significant aspects of our peculiarities, structured following early incidents that have been bound together in constant conjunction[3] that pursue no other purpose than to repeat the status quo; they are experiences inflicted by chance and repeated by compulsion. In other words, pre-conceptual traumas that take place in the first years of life are decisive in the shaping of our future personal-ity, determining how we are, what we do, and even the kind of person we choose as a partner. This fatalistic outcome will be referred to as the mark of Cain.

CHAPTER TWO

Dictators' early traumas

In this book, we are attempting a comparison between the psychological circumstances present in the early life of two different groups of individuals: totalitarian leaders, group A, such as Stalin, Hitler, Mao, Castro, and Saddam; and Group B, consisting of very creative people, such as Picasso, Einstein, Gandhi, Beethoven, and Freud. When we initiated this investigation, we never imagined we were going to find so many childhood facts in common among the individuals in each group.

We have composed a table depicting the most relevant aspects found in comparing the two groups:

    i)   dead brothers before the birth of the individual;
   ii)   absence or presence of a father during the first years of life;
  iii) sequence of birth;
  iv) physical violence during childhood;
   v) emotional link between father and child;
  vi) difference or coincidence between trade or profession of fathers and sons;
 vii) significant feelings of revenge;
viii) socio-economic level.

Comparative table

Name	Legitimate or illegitimate	Dead siblings	Father: absent or present	Mother's age	Father's age	Birth order	Father's violence	Father's occupation	Mother's occupation	Acting, "Revengeful hope"	Son's occupation. Similar/different from father's	Social status
Che Guevara	L	0	Present	22	28	Oldest	No	Architect		Signific.	Dif.	Middle class
Stalin	L	2 prev.	Absent	20	29	3rd oldest	Significant	Cobbler	Maid	Signific.	Dif.	Poor
Hitler	I	3 prev.	Absent	28	51	4th oldest	Significant	Cobbler, Customs police	Maid	Signific.	Dif.	Poor
Mao	L	2 prev.	Absent	18	15	3rd oldest	Some	Peasant, Agricult.	Household	Signific.	Dif.	Poor
Castro	I	0	Absent	15	51	3rd oldest	Significant	Landowner	Maid	Signific.	Dif.	Poor (?)
Saddam	?	1 prev.	Absent stepfather	27	?	2nd oldest	Significant	Stepfather: burglar	?	Signific.	Dif.	Poor
Picasso	L	0	Present	26	43	Oldest	No	Artist	Household	Signific.	Same	Middle class
Gandhi	L	0	Present	25	47	4th youngest	No	Politician	Household	No	Same	Middle class
Beethoven	L	1 prev. 3 after	Present	21	28	2nd oldest	Some	Musician	Maid	Signific.	Same	Middle class
Freud	L	1	Present	21	41	Oldest	No	Businessman	Household	No	Dif.	Middle class

Child mortality rates were much higher in the past, which explains why there were more dead babies in the case of dictators, because they were older than those in the creative group, with the exception of Beethoven and Freud, who had dead brothers prior to their births, and Castro, who being more recent, did not have any. However, this issue of mortality is absolutely irrelevant to the purpose of our investigation, because what appears to be germane in this inquiry is the emotional consequences the loss of siblings seem to impose on the relationship between mothers and their living children. The death of the first child can be a painful blow for a young mother, who might, from then on, be haunted by the fear of losing the next one, consequently becoming excessively protective of those who have survived. She will then identify the dead child with the living one and treat the latter as if he or she is continuously on the verge of dying. The child, on his or her part, will sense the mother's concern as a form of fear and weakness that will induce a need to protect and look after her. All families from group A were of poor extraction, in comparison to those families from group B.

Group A

Keke Dzhughashvili, Joseph Stalin's mother

> smothered him with attention and affection … she never let him out of her sight till he was six years old … he had been a sickly infant. (Service, 2004, p. 19)

Keke had two other children before Stalin was born:

> the first was Mikhail, who died when only one year old. Then came Giorgi, but he too died young. Joseph alone survived early childhood. It might have been expected that Joseph's mother and father, having suffered the loss of two sons in infancy, would have treated their third with special care and affection. (Ibid., p. 16)

Perhaps this apprehension was sensed by Joseph as a form of weakness, something that could have induced in him the need to protect and look after her. In trying to save his life, the mother became very religious and insisted that Joseph enter the seminary to become a priest.

> [S]he made him feel special and dressed him as well as her finances allowed. Besarion [his father] resented this. Keke set her heart on Joseph becoming educated and entering the priesthood whereas Besarion wanted him to be a cobbler like himself. (Ibid.)

There is an account by one of Joseph's teachers at the time he entered the Gori Spiritual School in 1888. It is obvious from this portrayal that the mother took special care about how to dress him, and that she dressed him like a "little pseudo adult", perhaps "ageing" him in an unconscious attempt way to keep him alive ahead of time, in order to magically avoid the same fate of his previous brothers. Vano Ketskhoveli, the teacher, recalls:

> I ... saw that among the pupils was standing a boy I didn't know, dressed in a long *akhalukhi* [a plain, body-garment] which went down to his knees, in new boots with high tops. He had a thick leather belt tightly drawn around his waist. On his head was a black cloth peak-cap with a varnished peak which shone in the sun. (Ibid., pp. 20–21)

He continues:

> No one else wore either an *akhalukhi* or such boots, and the pupils pressed around him out of curiosity. Obviously his mother was very eager to dress her son as well as possible; she had coddled him since birth. She herself had never been to school, and probably she did not understand that by dressing him up differently, she did him no favours with his fellow pupils. Gradually he began to stand up to her ... (Ibid., p. 21)

Such preference, or "narcissistic identification", from the mother towards the surviving child can also be observed in Adolf Hitler's early years. Klara Hitler, in a matter of a few months, lost her first three children, all in infancy, and although Adolf was the first to survive, he also seemed sickly. Alois, his father, complained bitterly to his mother because he felt she had not borne him a healthy child. According to Victor (1998), the continuous aggression, mistreatment, and beating from her husband induced a sense of hopelessness, and since she felt powerless to change her own situation, she resorted to putting "her energies into raising a special child who, in turn, wanted to become a champion" (p. 21).

Klara believed Adolf had a weak constitution and she never stopped believing it. Because she was his caretaker, her perception affected him strongly. Adolf's health became her constant concern. She overprotected and overindulged him and favoured him over her stepchildren and her children born after him. Her belief that he was sickly and in need of special treatment would lead to him being allowed to drop out of school on the basis of a supposed lung disease. It would also foster the hypochondria he would suffer throughout his adult life.

Perhaps Hitler's resemblance with his mother, continues Victor,

> heightened her closeness to her special child. Reportedly Klara caressed him often and breast-fed him longer than her other children and, when Alois was away, took Adolf into her bed. Her intimacy with him was obvious to relatives and acquaintances. Bloch said, "I have never witnessed a closer attachment" and "One thing is certain: he idolized his mother …!" Klara's attachment to Adolf remained extreme until her death. (Ibid., p. 24)

And further on:

> A boy who is close to an abused mother tends to become her champion, to have fantasies about standing up for her, rescuing her, and providing a better life for her. As the child grows up, the fantasies often turn into the ambition to become a champion of the people. (Ibid., p. 29)

Some of these close ties to his mother were more obvious after she developed cancer:

> He took over her care, cooking for her, cleaning, and scrubbing the floor. He comforted and nursed her. According to Paula [his younger sister] "… Adolf spoiled my mother during this last time of her life with overflowing tenderness. He was indefatigable in his care for her, wanted to comply with any desire she could possibly have and did all to demonstrate his great love for her." [Dr] Bloch [the doctor who looked after her illness] said, "He would watch her every movement so that he might anticipate her slightest need. His eyes,

which usually gazed mournfully into the distance, would light up whenever she was relieved of her pain ..." For the rest of his life, Adolf kept a photograph of Klara with him, hanging over his bed, taking it along on trips, looking at it daily. (Ibid., pp. 40–41)

Mao's childhood history follows a similar dynamic. His two older brothers died before he was born, and attempting to avoid Mao following the same fate, his mother turned to her devotion to Buddha and made Mao her *Tse-tung*, from *Tse* signifying "to shine on" and *tung* "the East", or to "shine from the East", meaning to have a fortunate birth. Not satisfied with all these forms of protection Mao's mother also resorted to choosing, as was the habit at that time, a nickname that could guarantee toughness and strength—*Shi san ya-zi*, signifying "the Boy of Stone".

> For this second "baptism" his mother took him to a rock about eight feet high, which was reputed to be enchanted, as there was a spring underneath. After Mao performed obeisance and kowtows he was considered adopted by the rock. (Chang & Halliday, 2005, p. 5)

It is quite possible to conjecture from these accounts that, similar to the mothers of Stalin and Hitler, Mao's mother might also have established a close narcissistic tie with the surviving son. Such an attitude on the part of the mother, of being absolutely terrorised about the possibility of losing another child, could have been interpreted by the son as an expression of insecurity, fear, and complete dependency on his health; which could have been eventually translated into idealisation of sickness and, later on, into hypochondria. In this circumstance, the child could feel omnipotent, and absolutely indispensable to the well-being of his mother. The presence, at the same time, of very violent fathers, who continuously abused the vulnerability of these women, would not only induce in the boys the need to rescue their mothers, but also enhance the sense of absolute indispensability.

Saddam Hussein falls partly into this category, although with certain differences. When Subha was pregnant with Saddam, she lost her husband, Saddam's father, as well as her twelve-year-old son. She became so depressed and desperate that she first tried to abort and then to commit suicide, but was both times dissuaded from doing so by neighbours and friends. She called her son Saddam, meaning in Arabic "the one who confronts". However, a serious post-partum psychosis forced her to place Saddam with an uncle, where he stayed for the first four years of his life.

Another important aspect is the violence present in the majority of the fathers in the group of dictators. Klara, twenty-three years younger than, and a niece to, Alois Hitler, her husband—the only man in her life—was continuously abused by him. Over the years he became distant to the point of moving by himself to Linz, leaving the family behind. According to a friend of his, "Alois hardly saw his family at all". Given his history, it would have been only logical for Klara to assume he was having affairs. When he *was* with the family, Alois went daily to the tavern, often returning home in a bad mood. And at some time during the marriage, he reportedly began to beat Klara (Victor, 1998, p. 23).

A year later, after Alois had returned home from Linz, he found that Alois Jr., Adolf's older half-brother, was extremely disobedient and difficult to manage:

> A strict father, Alois was intolerant of disobedience, and he was moodier that before … The result was an intense clash of wills. Alois often beat Alois Jr., and, on catching him in truancy, choked him and nearly killed him. It was then that Alois Jr., left home— running away, according to his siblings; being forced out by his father, according to his own account. (Ibid., p. 28)

The account of beating Adolf, on the other hand, came from Paula, the younger sister, and was supported by Alois Jr.'s report. Adolf had escaped his father's brutality due to the presence of his half-brother who was used as the scapegoat, but when he ran away, Adolf became the target of his father's violence, who at that time according to Klara, "carried a whip in the house, terrifying the family" (ibid.).

> Overindulged [by his mother attention and overprotection], Adolf was unaccustomed to dealing with either frustration or punishment, let alone destructive anger. His siblings said he grew up determined to have his way. He had learned he could overcome his mother's objections by brightness, persuasion, stubbornness, or tantrums. But none of these worked with Alois … For the first time Adolf's omnipotence was challenged seriously and his weakness exposed. And it remained exposed, for Klara did not protect him

from his father … Adolf became very stubborn with his father and, according to his sister Paula, provocative. Probably the repetition of what happened with his first son was too much for Alois. Paula said he beat Adolf daily and severely. Then, at ten, Adolf decided to run away. On discovering this, Alois beat him so badly he went into a coma. For days the family did not know whether he would live. (Ibid., pp. 28–29)

Ibrahim al Hassan, Saddam Hussein's step-father, a petty thief nicknamed "the Liar", married Suba, his mother, after she became a widower when Saddam's father died of cancer at the time she was pregnant with him. Suba also lost her older son at the age of twelve while still pregnant with Saddam, developing such a state of depression and anxiety that she pulled clumps of hair out and hit her pregnant abdomen in despair. She was quoted as saying that after losing her husband and her child, "what good was it for her to have a new baby". She even tried to commit suicide by throwing herself in front of a bus but was deterred from doing so by some neighbours. Very early on, Ibrahim, her new husband, forced her to give up Saddam by sending him to stay with an uncle, until he was around five; he returned to stay with his mother because his uncle was in jail accused of conspiracy. Ibrahim, not being very fond of Saddam, mistreated him continuously, by whipping him in the street with a long stick as the child jumped to avoid being hit.

Lazy and cruel, the Liar used the boy to steal sheep from neighbouring farms, woke him every morning brutally pulling his hair while screaming, wake up son-of-a-bitch. (Myerson, 2000, p. 231)

After Saddam became the strong man of Iraq, and the family lived in great wealth, his stepfather was still living in a mud hut in the small and poor village of Uja.

Besarion, father to Joseph Stalin, also known by the nick name of "Mad Beso", was famous for his drunkenness and short temper. He frequently "flared up into angry violence against his wife" (Service, 2004, p. 16). Stalin once confessed to his daughter Svetlana,

how he stood up to his father and threw a knife at him when Keke was taking yet another beating. The knife missed its aim. Besarion hurled himself at young Joseph but was too slow to catch him.

> Joseph ran off and was hidden by neighbours until his father's rage
> had spent itself. (Ibid., p. 19)

Without exception, all his friends from that time remember that Beso was brutal to his son. What made things worse for Joseph's subsequent development was that his father's violence was neither merited nor predictable. It is scarcely astounding that he grew up with a strong tendency towards resentment and retaliation (ibid.).

One of Stalin's favourite books was Alexander Qazbegi's novel *The Parricide*, in which "Koba", the main character, declares that "revenge is sweet" and that he will "always pursue to the death those who have wronged them [the *abreks*, of which Koba was one]. Koba declares: 'I'll make their mothers weep!'" (ibid., p. 28). Koba became Stalin's God and the meaning of his life. "From then onwards he called himself Koba, he absolutely didn't want us to call him any other name" (ibid.).

Cruelty touched Castro in a different form. There were no previous dead brothers, nor was he the older son; however, in common with the others was his father's violence and an adolescent mother, reliant and illiterate. His life history is primarily about separation, total desertion from both parents, scorn, physical abuse from tutors, classmates, and the Jesuits in the boarding school where he stayed for many years. He was the third illegitimate son of Angel Castro, a Gallego immigrant and illiterate, who eventually became a rich Cuban landowner.

Angel Castro married Maria Luisa Argota, the teacher who taught him how to read and write, and had two children with her. At the age of fifty he seduced Lina Ruz, who was fourteen years old (the same age as his eldest daughter) and of mixed heritage. After he had three children with Lina (Angela, Ramon, and Fidel), Maria Luisa asked for a divorce and demanded half of Angel's possessions, who then declared bankruptcy and sent Lina and their children away to avoid being indicted. They ended up living with Lina's mother in a miserable hut, very far from Angel's main residence. He continued visiting in secret, and three more children were born: Raul, Juana, and Enma. Because they were "conceived in sin" the church refused to baptise them, which troubled Lina enormously. Later on, this condition became a reason for scorn and mockery when other children accused Fidel of being a Jew, and often ended in coming to blows.

When Fidel was four year old, he was send to live with the Hypolites, a couple of Haitian slave drivers without any scruples, who favoured physical punishment, "beat children and did not allowed any noise while in their presence" (Raffy, 2004, p. 27). Three years later, when he was seven, Fidel was placed in a boarding school run by priests, who accepted him reluctantly and under the influence of a friend, because he was not baptised. During holidays, he was allowed to visit his mother at her hut, but never his father at the big house. Over the years he became very impressionable:

> He could not stand any injustice, aggressively addressed teachers who showed preference for other pupils and often was punished because of that. He was angry against the friars who only seemed to favour the children from the aristocracy. Should he scream at these self-satisfied pretentious burgesses, who not only were baptized, but also, whose mothers knew how to read and write and what was even worst, had never lived in a hut. (Ibid., p. 35)

When finally he was baptised, with the purpose of the relationship with his father as well as his illegitimacy continuing to be hidden, he was registered as "Fidel Hypolite", as if the Haitian who represented him were his true father. Fidel grew up feeling absolutely alien: to a college of rich people where he boarded for years, and with the family he never had. He was, together with his other siblings, the *corpus delicti* of his parent's marital infidelity that it was necessary to hide. He grew up full of resentment, envy, and revengeful hope against his powerful father, while at the same time he tried to protect his defenceless mother and grandmother.

> He resented the whole world: his family who had abandoned him in the clutches of Luis Hypolite, whose name he had but hated; the friars who did not appreciate him and had never accepted him; his classmates with whom he felt irremediably different because he lacked their good manners. (Ibid., p. 38)

Conclusion

We consider that the traumas found in the biographies of individuals from this group present the following characteristics: i) significant cruelty and extreme violence from the father, or stepfather, as observed in the case of Hussein; ii) young dependent mothers who were also similarly abused; iii) death of previous children, making the child in question as if the elder, with the exception of Castro; iv) narcissistic attachment of the mother to the child, inducing in him the feeling that she is in total distress and in need of being rescued, and as a consequence, the feeling that he ought to be her "true saviour"; v) extreme poverty; vi) there were all boys.

In the previous chapter devoted to "trauma" we referred to how children deal with painful traumatic events by mentally fragmenting them (atomising) and continuously projecting them outside. This is why these traumatic events remain unconsciously extremely active, very often determining the total profile of an individual character and demeanour. One of us also referred to this aspect as Cain's mark (López-Corvo, 2014). Many will dispute the importance of these variables, on the basis that our argument is biased, suffering from psychological reductionism, presenting only one point of view, and neglecting the relevance of social matters, for instance.

Group B

Individuals in this group came mostly from the middle class, and, with the exception of Beethoven, none had dead siblings before their birth. Also, different from group A, in all these families the fathers were always present, usually of similar professions, and never acted out aggression against the mothers or the children. Picasso's father, for instance, was a painter like himself; Beethoven's father and grandfather were also musicians; and Gandhi father's was also a politician. Einstein's father had an inclination towards physics and created a company with his brother, who was an engineer, to provide telephone and electrical services. Freud was the only one who, as a medical doctor, had a profession different from his father, who was a fur trader. Mothers from this group appeared more independent: Einstein's mother, for instance, was an artist and pianist; Maria Picasso López is described in her son's biography (Richardson, 1991) as "strong, tender and typically Andalusian"—different from her husband, who is described as "weak and affectionate". With the exception of Gandhi they were all older children.

Creativity in group A

Marilou Gjermes, art curator of the USA army, observing some pictures painted by Hitler, argued that the Second World War and the Holocaust would have never happened had Hitler been accepted by Vienna's art school and become an architect (López-Corvo, 2014, p. 285). Unfortunately, the mind does not function in such a simple manner, because the terror experienced by Hitler during his first years of life as a consequence of his father's exaggerated violence, as well as the presence of a terribly diminished adolescent mother, induced in him the imperative paranoid need to project outside a threatening inner element in order to fight, overpower, and finally destroy it ad infinitum. In these circumstances, a mental development towards the creation and production of art, as we could see in a painter, would have been absolutely impossible. In other words, only if Hitler had been murdered would the Second World War and the Holocaust never have taken place.

Narcissistic structure of the mother

Freud described as "phallic envy" those emotions women experience toward the greater freedom and privilege that culture has universally provided men with; a difference that has generally focused on that between the vagina and the penis. However, the truth is that men and women equally have to deal in life with important feelings of absence, or "castration anxiety" as we usually refer to it in analytical terms. In order to compensate for the "narcissistic fault" of not having a penis, of not having the privileges men seem to display, Freud described women, in having a baby, as employing the formula "baby = penis = faeces". Compensations made by mothers using the fantasy of a "faecal phallus" are dynamics we find most of the time in drug abuse (López-Corvo, 1993, 2014). Men, on the other hand, deal with absences by means of rivalry and competition, as we see in wars, for instance. Very often, mothers, in order to compensate for their own absence, favour a child, often a boy, who is usually chosen according to a series of variables: being a boy, the older, the taller, the handsomer, and so on, a condition that was present in most of the cases in group A.

CHAPTER THREE

Communism as a form of psychopathology

> Socialism is a philosophy of failure, the creed of ignorance, and the gospel of envy, its inherent virtue is the equal sharing of misery.
>
> —Winston Churchill

We have not found, so far, a satisfactory psychoanalytical reference for the evaluation and understanding of totalitarian or tyrannical regimes (Šebek, 1996). This is why we have decided to venture into the evaluation of a close psychoanalytic profile of those well-known dictators who have being responsible for millions and millions of deaths around the world, and who are still desecrating, plundering, killing, and terrorising defenceless populations; as has been the case in Stalin's Russia, Hitler's Germany, Mussolini's Italy, Peron's Argentina, Franco's Spain, Mao's China, Pinochet's Chile, Chauchesco's Rumania, Castro's Cuba, and Milosevic's Yugoslavia, just to mention some of the more modern ones.

"Tyranny" is not "a habit capable of being developed, and at last becomes a disease", as Dostoyevsky once stated; tyranny—we say—is, from the very beginning, not just a disease but a deadly pandemic. The problem, ultimately, is that the Platonic configuration of ideal social systems can only be put into practice by the *mind* of certain individuals—as we have seen in previous chapters—who, due to their own idiosyncrasies, identify with such a system and exercise its model within the limits of their own possibilities, with the sole purpose of satisfying their own egotistical desires. After all, as Protagoras once stated, "of all things the measure is Man, of the things that are, for what they are, and of the things that are not, for what they are not". The dictator is acting not so much on the need of people, but on the need to put into practice, and to act out, inner and private childhood fantasies usually related to authoritarian fathers and seductive mothers. In attempting this exercise of finding a psychic explanation of tyranny, we have used a form of psychoanalytic approach known in the field as "object relations", based mainly on the contributions of Melanie Klein, Donald Meltzer, and Wilfred Bion.

Totalitarian regimes implemented to extremes, as in Nazi Germany, in the late Soviet Union, or in present-day Cuba, represent a form of unconscious psychopathology acted out by certain "leaders" as well as by followers. These are individuals who have identified with this form of political system because of painful childhood experiences, which can be recognised in their biographies with uncanny coincidence, regardless of time and culture. The main consequences of these early experiences are feelings of exclusion, paranoia, anger, destructive envy, hope based on revenge, and a powerful need to conceive of themselves as "essential" to the well-being of their mothers when they are children, or of the country when they become adults. Historically, all totalitarian systems have been imposed by men, and never by women, an issue we will elaborate on later.

Tyrannical regimes are alike because the main aim of the system is the need to put into practice, at any cost, the private, omnipotent, and megalomaniac fantasies of the leader. There is the psychotic delusion that the country is in immediate need of urgent rescue by a saviour, a hero who will protect it from an immediate danger, will fix and straighten out all the wrong-doing carelessly and incompetently exercised by inept predecessors. This is a need similar to that experienced as a child, to rescue mother from the cruelty and violence of father. In order to endlessly repeat this condition, they have developed the psychotic desire for complete indispensability, and in order to put this into practice and to remain indispensable, the country must continuously be on the verge of collapse and in need of "intensive care". Such an operation demands complete control of political, legal, social, and economic aspects of the country. Control is necessary in order to implement the leader's private will and the need to exercise his determining fantasies. As we shall see further on, control is unconsciously dogged by infantile anal concerns.

Any opposition or interference in the implementation of such a fantasy is considered by the totalitarian regime as a threat to the continuity of power and will be attacked relentlessly and viciously, inducing persecution, physical disappearance of dissenters, and absolute terror. Indispensability is sensed as an "all or nothing" kind of interaction, of life or death, essential or disposable, and nothing in-between. There are three main fears: a) that somebody else could be a better rescuer or be considered more essential than the totalitarian leader; b) that the leader's true "personal intentions" of destructive envy and hopeless revenge will be revealed; and c) that the leader is no longer essential. This last apprehension might be sensed by the tyrant but can never be experienced.

In order to camouflage the true personal and pathological intention to overpower other human beings, and to exercise a perverse private fantasy of control and sadism, totalitarian systems will continuously require a massive display of propaganda, because there is always the terror of discovering that the true personal intentions of the tyrant have nothing to do with the true needs of the country. If the intentions of the totalitarian leader were sincerely directed towards the well-being of the people, there would be no fear about any form of criticism; indeed it would be welcome because such criticism would help to make corrections toward the achievement of such a purpose. Terror about criticism simply implies that there are other private, wicked, and hidden purposes, which are different from those necessary to help the people.

Equally, at the other end of the spectrum, "savage capitalism", as we shall see in the next chapter, represents the expression of similar inner conflicts in those who compulsively make a cult of the power of money. While communist leaders will decree "social unfairness due to uneven distribution of wealth" capitalists will use the "absence of freedom" in order to implement the power of riches. What I am stating now should be of no surprise to anyone, particularly the fact that the very early years of life are always profoundly and fatalistically determinant of future behaviour. It has been said that Columbus did not discover America, but invented it; it was in his head even before he arrived in the New World. Serial killers are similarly paradigmatic; behavioural researchers understand that explanations of their murders can be found within the obscure and difficult years of their childhood, usually in the psychological profile of their relationship with their siblings and parents, primarily the mothers. In certain individuals early psychological traumas induce powerful fantasies, which continuously but unconsciously demand realisation. Such early fantasies can become a central and decisive pattern that will unconsciously determine certain forms of adult demeanour. This might be considered to be a form of "psychologism" or psychoanalytic reductionism that leaves out other issues more apparent and of "greater" relevance. An artificial dichotomy between the "individual" and the "group" in relation to totalitarianism has already been introduced by Popper (1971), who opposed what he calls "methodological individualism" to "methodological collectivism". The problem with this argument is that John Stuart Mill's book, *A System of Logic*, used by Popper for his argumentation, was published in 1875, long before Bion's experiments with group psychology in the 1950s had taken place.

Marx himself opposed "psychologism" by insisting on "sociologism", as can be observed in his statement that "it is not the consciousness of man that determines his existence—rather, it is his social existence that determines his consciousness". Marx could have responded to Hegel's influence, of what could be conceived as "Hegel's Platonising collectivism", where the state and the nation are more "real" than the individual who owes everything to them. We know now that such Manichaeism between what is "social" and what is "individual" makes no sense, that the individual will influence the group in the same fashion that the group will influence the individual. Wilfred Bion (1948) clearly proved, following his experiments with "leaderless groups", that the group and the leader interact according to three universal possibilities he described as "basic assumptions", which we will be referring to in detail in Chapter Five.

What I want to convey is that Marx's point of view, that the problems of society are irreducible to those of human nature, is exactly where Marx's failure, and the failure of communism as the solution for global poverty, hinges. The utopian naïveté present in the *The Communist Manifesto* contrasts with the wicked selfishness present in those men who try to implement it. However, regardless of that incongruity, the true fact is that no other philosopher has ever influenced humanity to such an extent; the world has never been the same since Karl Marx.

Marx and Engels became influenced by Hegel's theory of the evolving process of history, which was based on "correlation" of differences, meaning that things or thoughts exist interrelated to their opposites, in the sense that dark is correlated with light, good with bad, master with slave, and so on. Hegel also argued that "unity" could only be achieved by the levelling of all the opposites, by means of dialectic and logical progression of thesis, antithesis, and synthesis. For instance, to "comply" (thesis) and to "rebel" (antithesis) are often two sides of the same coin (synthesis); or in the dialectic of "master-slave," the "master" (thesis) could become "slave" (antithesis) to his darling's love (synthesis), while "slave" could transcend material dependency and achieve a state of inner freedom (synthesis). Engel and Marx coined the term "historical materialism", where the main cause and engine of all historical change would be based on economic grounds, in the changes of form of production and exchange within the struggle of classes between the bourgeoisie (thesis) and proletariat (antithesis); a dialectic that could only be solved, they said, by means of communism (synthesis). In Part II of *The Communist Manifesto* they declare that the intention of communism was to overthrow the bourgeoisie and to situate all political power in the hands of proletariat. Different from other philosophers, Marx was not interested in finding the ultimate truth and understanding of the world, but in changing it. Although he honestly believed in what he preached, there have been two devastating consequences of his theories: one relates to the impossibility of implementation of an economy solely based on and dependent on the state; second, and more importantly, those who attempt to put communism into practice respond to their own obscure narcissistic needs of despotism, extreme envy, and murder.

Che Guevara

Let us take, for instance, Ernesto "Che" Guevara (1928–1967), a legendary leftist whose early death changed him into a hero and a universal myth. He was the eldest child of an Argentinean upper middle class family. Celia de la Serna y Llosa (1906–1965), his mother, was an orphan from an early age—her father committed suicide when she was two and her mother died when she was fifteen—a condition that would have induced in her a great sense of loss, loneliness, and a significant need for affection. For someone who had lost both of her parents the birth of a child could have represented a "true blood relation", a replacement for her lost parents, quite different from the "political relation" she had with her husband.

Described as a "loner" and "aloof" (Anderson, 1997), perhaps as a form of emotional withdrawal from others in order to protect herself from further lost and pain, she might have experienced her son as a narcissistic extension of herself, her only "true possession". Such a narcissistic need could very well explain why Che Guevara suffered from asthma from the age of one. Asthma can result from a close, overprotective, and suffocating relationship with the mother, which induces oedipal conflicts, amongst them sexual inhibition such as sexual impotence (Adroer, 1996; Racker, 1948). Led by Celia, the Guevara family continuously rambled around the country in search of drier climates, avoiding humidity, supervising what Ernesto ate and did in order to alleviate his asthma attacks. Ernesto did not attend school until he was nine years old, and only because the police forced his mother to send him. "This period," says Anderson, "undoubtedly consolidated the special relationship that had already formed between them." The symbiosis between them was to "acquire dramatic resonance in the years ahead as they sustained their relationship through a rich flow of soul-bearing correspondence that lasted until Celia's death in 1965" (p. 17). However, often in spite of all the efforts, "Ernesto was carried out prostrated and wheezing by his friends" (ibid., p. 18).

Such a close relationship with his mother resulted not only in asthma, but also in dependency, fear, frustration, and anger. Che's father, on the other hand, who was accused of being unfaithful, became depressed after failing in several endeavours that left him jobless and financially dependent on his well-to-do wife. Photographs from that time show Celia as a hard-looking woman, almost masculine; while her husband, Ernesto Guevara Lynch, appears soft and rather feminine. An important role of fathers, within the psychological dynamics of any family, is their role as a "rescuer" of children from the mother's natural gravitational symbiosis. A soft father, together with an overpowering mother, will obviously result in enhancement and furtherance of the symbiotic ties toward the mother and as a consequence, if there is a genetic predisposition, the appearance of a somatic ailment such as asthma. As compensation for such dependency, opposite feelings are also induced, something referred to by psychopathology as "reaction formation" or "counter-phobic" mechanisms. At school Ernesto did anything to get attention and to master his fears; he drank ink, ate chalk, climbed trees, and dangerously explored mine shafts. Later on, after becoming a commandant with Castro's rebels in Cuba, he turned into a dangerous and callous executioner, as has been reported by Cubans who fought on his side. Perhaps he became a doctor in an attempt to deal with his illness, and a guerrilla fighter to deal with his fear. In other words, Che's mind was split in two: on one hand there was an "asthmatic aspect", a child-like need for dependency and fear—which could have been identified with cowardice—while on the other hand there were tough overcompensating attempts to hide these fears, perceived as understood as bravery. He fought with Castro during the invasion of Cuba's, ruthlessly killing peasants accused of being government allies, the very people they said they were liberating from the "regime's oppression". Recently, in a television programme, the son of an army captain angrily accused Che of killing his father during an interrogation that took place in his office. "He stood up and walked around the room, went behind my father who was sitting tied to a chair, pulled out gun and shot him twice in his head."

In an article, "Che Guevara, the killing machine", in *El País* in Spain, Alvaro Vargas Llosa (2005), stated:

> Guevara's disposition, when he travelled with Castro, from Mexico to Cuba in the Granma, is reflected in the phrase of a letter written to his wife on the 28th of January, 1957, shortly after disembarking, that later was published in his book: Memories del Che Guevara en Sierra Maestra. There he said: "Here, in Cuba's jungle, I live thirsty of blood."

And further on:

> In January 1957, as stated in his diary from Sierra Maestra, Guevara killed Eutimio Guerra just with one shot, because he suspected that he was passing information to the enemy: "I finished the problem with a calibre 32 gun on the right side of his brain. ... His belongings are mine now." Afterwards he shot Aristidio, a peasant who expressed his wish to abandon the fight at the time the rebels were moving to another place. While he was asking himself if this victim in concrete "was really sufficiently guilty to deserve that," his hands did not shake at the time he order Echeverria's murder, the brother of one of his comrades, because of unspecified crimes: "he had to pay the price." On other occasions he simulated executions although he might not carry them out, just as a form of psychological torture.

And also:

> ... many persons were murdered in the Cabaña? Pedro Corzo pro-
> vided a number of around 200, similar to those offered by Armando
> Lago, a retired professor of economy who has elaborated a list of
> around 179 names, as part of a study on executions that took place
> in Cuba. In secret messages sent by the American Embassy to the
> state Department in Washington from La Habana, they referred to
> "more than 500" executions.

At his execution in Vallegrande, Bolivia, possibly attempting to hide his
fear, Che exclaimed in macho fashion to his executioner: "Shoot, cow-
ards, you're only going to kill a man."

Such a personality structure and unconscious dynamic profile is
completely different from those found in "totalitarian dictators" such
as Castro, Mao, Hitler, or Stalin, as we shall see further on, who instead
responded to an unconscious need to "possess" and "control". Che was
narcissistically completely compromised in the attempt to prove to himself and to others that he was not the frightened child—or the coward—
that he sensed he was. Guerrilla war, where he could continuously
prove to himself that he was not a "frightened coward"[1] was the essential enterprise that was his main concern, which is why he presented
himself as someone completely unconcerned about earthly possessions.
He gave up all those duties—such as being President of the Central
Bank—that Castro requested him to perform in "liberated" Cuba, as he
preferred to continue fighting, first in Africa and later in Bolivia. He was
clearly not interested in attaching himself to the land that he by then
considered free. On 3 October 1965, Castro read to the public a letter of
farewell sent by Che:

> "I feel that I have fulfilled the part of my duty that tied me to the
> Cuban revolution in its territory. And I say goodbye to you, the
> comrades, and your people, who are already mine ... Other nations
> of the world call for my modest efforts. I can do that which is denied
> to you because of your responsibility as the head of Cuba, and the
> time has come for us to part."

There is no question that he was doomed, from very early on, to die in
the manner in which he did.

What we are stating, in other words, is a form of solipsistic approach, where the mind, as Protagoras once stated, "is the measure of all things", meaning that men are fatalistically bound to the limitations of their mind, to the restrictions of their past, unless, with the use of appropriate means, they become aware and manage to overcome the burden and compulsions of their own history. This, as we have stated previously, can appear as a form of psychoanalytic reductionism, attempting to explain adult "social" behaviour as a direct consequence of early traumatic events. We are not stating that this form of research denies that these individuals possess other more altruistic interests; on the contrary, what we are trying to express is how the individual's psychological and idio-syncratic profile can divert such altruism into more selfish and egoistic aims that disregard the needs of other people. For instance, Castro could have been motivated at the beginning of his revolution, at the time he fought Batista's dictatorship, by sincere concern for the Cuban people, their poverty and suffering; however, almost fifty years later, he is clearly driven by revenge, sadism, and the need to control, and is power hunger, which has changed him into yet another incompetent and dan-gerous dictator, even worse than Batista. Mao on the other hand, never referred to poor peasants at the beginning of his struggle as a commu-nist and never cared what became of his abandoned wives and children. In their book, *Mao, the Unknown Story*, Chang and Halliday (2005) state:

> Mao's attitude to morality consisted of one core, the self, "I", above everything else: "I do not agree with the view that to be moral, the motive of one's action has to be benefiting to others. Morality does not have to be defined in relation to others … Of course there are people and objects in the world, but they are all there for me … People like me only have a duty to ourselves; we have no duty to other people." (p. 13)

Mao had little concern for peasants and the poor:

> There is no sign that Mao derived from his peasant roots any social concerns, much less that he was motivated by a sense of injustice … Mao's peasant background did not imbue him with idealism about improving the lot of Chinese peasants. (pp. 8–9)
> He felt no more sympathy for workers than he did for peasants. (p. 30)

Any opposition from sensible and logical people, who have under-standing, will be experienced as a threat to the integrity of the imposed system and will trigger the leader's paranoia, inducing persecution and the disappearance of dissenters as well as an endless supply of misinfor-mation, usually based on lies, in order to camouflage the true personal and pathological need to controlling others in order to exercise private fantasy. The unconscious intentions that drive the leader are different from those of the followers.

CHAPTER FOUR

Capitalism: another form of psychopathology

> The day the rich sees how the poor lives, and the poor knows how rich works, the world will change.
>
> —Aristotle Onassis (personal communication)

Definition

From a purely economic point of view, we could define capitalism as an economic system based on production by means of private owner-ship and free endeavour, according to a free interplay between supply and demand, and where profit is obtained by investment of capital and employment of labour. Over a century and half ago, Marx and Engel, in *The Communist Manifesto*, stated that

> [t]he bourgeoisie, wherever it has got the upper hand, has put an end to all feudal, patriarchal, idyllic relations. It has pitilessly torn asunder the motley feudal ties that bound man to his "natural superiors," and has left no other nexus between people than naked self-interest, than callous "cash payment." It has drowned out the most heavenly ecstasies of religious fervour, of chivalrous enthu-siasm, of philistine sentimentalism, in the icy water of egotistical

calculation. It has resolved personal worth into exchange value, and in place of the numberless indefeasible chartered freedoms, has set up that single, unconscionable freedom—Free Trade. In one word, for exploitation, veiled by religious and political illusions, it has substituted naked, shameless, direct, brutal exploitation. (1848, Chapter One)

Marx introduced a more humanised definition, adding a different dimension to those descriptions based on pure economic and impersonal terms. However, this "human" factor represents a crucial aspect that cannot be ignored when the evaluation of any capitalistic system is considered. From this point of view, capitalism means, in simple terms, to privilege money over any other human need, where money and the power of purchasing and consuming material goods override humanity. Marx used the concept of "alienation" to explain how workers become alien from the commodity they produce, "that the worker is related to the product of labour as to an alien object" (ibid.). Although this notion has validity in explaining some of the complications of capitalism, I feel Marx lacked the psychological awareness necessary to understand such a concept in depth. The consumer capitalist society relies heavily on continuous expenditure on commodities and it is basically and unconsciously dependent on the conviction that love is conditional, that we are only of value for what we "have" and never for what we "are". This is the result of a confusion between animate beings and inanimate things, or, in other words, from not harbouring inside a true sense of "unconditional love and concern".

Money as a form of perversion

Money has flowed through time as a process of abstraction and symbolisation, similar to language. Initially, currency had an intrinsic value according to the weight of coinage manufactured from what was considered precious metal. Later in history, as the world became more stable, legal tenders and bank notes appeared, which similarly to words (in the form of books), represented a general consensus about their equivalence in a value backed up by gold, not in the money itself, but in the specific country's bank. This consensus is based on trust, similar to that which allows someone to remain calm when a loved one is not present; the person relies on the confidence placed in the abstract representation that has been made of the other in the mind, because even if that person is not present, he or she still exists. Money, then, as we know it at present—coins, paper, plastic money, and so on—represents a symbolic account of labour; however, there is sufficient trust in its use that we accept it without hesitation, in spite of the absence of its equivalence in gold. In other words, just like the mental representation of loved ones, money, in whatever form, carries within it a symbolic shadow of truth and trust.

From a psychological point of view, any condition capable of interfering with mechanisms of symbolisation will have serious consequences on the individual's mind, ranging from addiction to psychosis. In psychosis, for instance, there is an absolute incapacity to differentiate "words" from "things". Words acquire a concrete meaning, in the sense that they no longer constitute a vehicle that points to meaning, but become the meaning itself. For instance, if someone were to say that I am poor and somebody else that I am rich, it will make no difference, because the truth depends not on the words themselves but strictly on the size of the capital I possess. But if I were to feel insulted by someone saying I am poor, or flattered by them saying I am rich, I will then be confusing "words" with "facts" in a perverse manner. It would be like thinking that just by saying that the "red fire truck" is white, it will change colour. In this sense we can say that this form of concrete thinking, where words are confused with facts, is a kind of "perversion", because instead of language representing a means, where communication is the end and the intention, it becomes an end in itself. In other words, the purpose of language as a form of communication is being perverted.

In capitalist societies, which depend on the permanent acquisition of new commodities, there is a constant group pressure, mostly from the media, to purchase the latest goods or face the risk of being left out, of becoming *démodé*. People judge others, and themselves, according to what they have, to how they appear, and not for what they are. Although this situation represents a source of suffering, particularly for those who have limited income, such pressure to obtain things and accumulate them in order to be happy keeps the economy buoyant. But a price is being paid: the individual, his desires and idiosyncrasies, are less relevant than that which is most important, and always more so than the person himself—that is, how much he is worth. There is an infinitude of "legal" hoaxes constantly being employed with the purpose of increasing expenditure and inducing debt, such as "buy

now pay later", countless credit cards, small print, endless bombard-
ment through the media, by telephone, or any form of mail, incessant
advertisement of bargains in order to hide swindles, and so on. In the
USA the term "the American dream" epitomises this attitude, where
the main purpose of life is not to "feel well", nor to be "at peace with
yourself", but to make and hoard money without any other consideration, until becoming "filthy rich", portrayed in the mythology of Walt
Disney in the character of *Scrooge McDuck*. As in psychosis, money is no
longer a means to a state of well-being, but an end in itself and the main
purpose of life. Similar to concrete thinking, this shift represents a form
of perversion of the true meaning of capital.

There are, however, serious consequences to this philosophy of life,
such as crime and violence, but most significantly, crimes committed
at a distance, to unknown individuals, such as the meaningless acts of
serial killers[1] or mass murderers.

Economy, geography, and the war against the elements

Why are countries with better economies located in the northern hemisphere, while "underdeveloped" nations are either equatorial or in the
southern hemisphere? If we look at a globe, we will see that land in
the northern hemisphere is much closer to the North Pole than land in
the southern hemisphere is to the South Pole. Northern territories are
not only more populated but are also much more exposed to extreme
temperatures than those such as Chile and Argentina at the tip of South
America, or South Africa on the other side of the earth. Extreme temperatures, mostly during the winter, present the difficulty of managing
long periods of low temperatures; there is also a real threat to human
life, less so at the present time, when there are many means of protection against the cold, but certainly until not too long ago when there
were few options to rely on. These countries are continuously at war
with the elements.

How can mothers help their children face such danger? They teach
them, among numerous other things, what to do in order to keep themselves warm, how to be resourceful and strong and not to be frail or
dependent. But what can a child do in order to be strong? Not to lament
or cry but to show firmness and determination, which implies not
being emotional. Feelings, then, became something not only dangerous but also shameful, a true expression of a weakness that must be

concealed. Such an attitude induces a form of culture we have referred to as "robotphilia", or the idealisation of machines, the desire to act, think, talk, and even dance like a robot; there is even a sophisticated name for it: "alexithymia", meaning "not having words for emotions". To equatorial inhabitants, northern people appear cold and autistic. As a consequence of not being comfortable showing their feelings to each other, people remain aloof and emotionless; and to the neophyte, they may appear distant and cold. But people are human, which means they have feelings in spite of how shameful they might feel about them, or how hard they might try to conceal, deny, project, or repress them; their emotions will always be there, regardless. So, what can they do when they feel blue, hopeless, or lonely? Well, they buy things, all sorts of commodities that will make them feel better, and the shopping malls will be full every weekend of people looking for new gadgets, while their garbage is being filled with the old ones they have to get rid of. But, most importantly, the economy will be booming. In the tropics, on the other hand, the weather not being so threatening means that leisure can be exercised without any real threat. People spend more time talking, and emotions are not so threatening, but the economy can never be as buoyant as it is in northern countries.

It is quite possible that some will consider these reflections an over-simplification of economic facts. However, I would like to alert the reader to the fact that I am only emphasising the psychological aspects, and leaving others for the experts in financial matters. Our thesis is not economic but based on human emotions. One of Marx's failures in terms of communism, for instance, could have been based on not understanding that natural leftist leaders have always harboured feelings of envy and revenge much stronger than the need to achieve freedom for the proletariat. Capitalism, on the other hand, is immensely hypocritical, because there is always the need to entice you to buy things. It is not interested in you as an individual, but in your pocket. At the same time, however, it has to make you believe that you are considered important, that it is really interested in you, and that you are not just an instrument to be used to get to your money. There is usually the feeling of the existence of an implicit world of "legal lies".

CHAPTER FIVE

The acolytes

There is a special place in Hell for those who remain silent.

—Dante Alighieri

In general, we can attempt to classify leadership into two kinds: i) narcissistic and dissociated leaders; ii) creative and integrative leaders. The first category corresponds to individuals driven absolutely by their own egoistic needs that never reflect the true desires of those they attempt to lead and is the group of dictators we will be referring to in this book. The second represents those leaders capable of sacrificing themselves for a cause that primarily benefits their people; we can think of Gandhi as a paradigm. Narcissistic leaders, as we have stated before, are always afraid of being discovered and accused of their true intentions, something that induces feelings of paranoia, a great sensitivity to what is said, and a powerful need to be always in control. The biographies of these tyrants are crammed with good examples.

It was common knowledge that Fidel Castro and Pablo Neruda had a mutual dislike and sometimes experienced uncomfortable encounters. Jorge Edwards (1993), a poet friend of Neruda, stated that he knew about such episodes after becoming Chile's ambassador to Cuba and that he was aware of them from Neruda, although never from Castro.

"One afternoon," remarked Edwards, "in the seventies, I don't remember the exact date, during an official reception on *La Esmeralda*, a boat which had just arrived in Havana, the Captain gave Fidel a book of Chilean poets. He started to examine it, sees a poem from Nicanor Parra and Castro made a comment, sees another poem from Gabriela Mistral and Fidel tells a joke … but when he arrived at Neruda's page, he looked at the poem, remains silent, and then turns the page. It was obvious to all the people present, his dislike and discomfort …" (Edwards, 1993, p. 36). What was the reason for such rancour? It was thought that when Neruda came to Cuba for the first time in 1960, he brought a book, *Canción de gesta*, in which he paid tribute to the Cuban revolution. It was believed that the relationship with Fidel became conflictual because a poem in that book dared to remind Castro that a revolution is similar to the making of a bottle of wine: it comprises the collective labour of many men working together, and not just one. In the poem, Neruda states that he has brought Castro a cup of wine from Chile. "Filled with so many hopes/that once you drink it, you will know that your victory/is like the old wine from my fatherland:/it is not made by one but by many men/and not from one grape but from many plants/it is not a drop but many rivers:/not a captain but many battles …" The resentment, as well as the complete control that Fidel Castro exercised over the Cuban intelligentsia, became obvious six years later, when under his direct orders a letter signed by one hundred Cuban writers was published in *Granma*—the party newspaper—condemning Neruda for accepting an invitation from his friend Arthur Miller to read "anti-imperialist" poems at the PEN congress in New York. Neruda never visited the island again.

There is a Spanish proverb that states: "For a sample, one button is enough." The fact that such insignificant remarks turned into a source of bitterness and were borne as an eternal grudge, clearly shows how important the narcissistic cult of the personality is to a totalitarian dictator. This is precisely the main difficulty supporters surrounding a tyrant have to face—that the leader's immense vulnerability to unconscious "childhood sibling rivalry" and absolute terror about being displaced, demands total surrender and complete absence of initiative. Since the only "creative" mind is that of the tyrant, there will be utter dread among the group of followers of producing ideas unilaterally, and more terrifying, of taking unilateral decisions, even if the urgency of a situation demands prompt intervention. This is a game that is very much present in the minds of small children, who believe that anything that moves is alive, even if it is powered by mechanical means, and will always prefer inanimate objects such as dolls or static toys that can be manipulated and controlled to their own desire. The minds of tyrants are full of this form of childish thinking, where independent and creative spirit induces uncertainty and pure terror.

Raffy (2004) narrates how during the sixties, because of the total deterioration of the Cuban economy, Castro imported the French agricultural engineer René Dumond to help with sugar cane production. At one point, because Dumond complained about some of Castro's methods, Fidel declared him persona non grata and expelled him from the island (pp. 372, 375).

For a while Molotov and Kaganovich were Stalin's watch dogs. They referred to him as the *Khozyain*, the "boss," and were absolutely compliant to the dictator's smallest whim. Although Molotov lacked the "gift of a strategist", Stalin promoted him to significant positions in the party, merely because he knew "that Molotov would loyally carry out the tasks given to him" (Service, 2004, p. 278). Service continues:

> He [Stalin] drove his ideas like iron into the minds of his associates … his implicit objectives was to form a fanatical Kremlin gang devoted to himself … Anyone who got in his way was expelled. In October 1930 he took offence at the People's Commissar for Finances. He wrote to the Politburo ordering: "Hang Bryukhanov by the balls for all his present and future sins. If his balls hold out, consider him acquitted in court; if they don't hold out, drown him in the river." (p. 280)

The purpose of the Great Terror Stalin set in train during the years 1937 to 1938 was to force intellectuals—meaning creative and independent minds—either to cooperate with the regime by keeping their heads down, to be exiled to the Gulag, or to die. Others, who had minds of their own, such as Trotsky, had to flee for their lives. Nikolai Yezhov, for instance—an alcoholic and sexual dissolute—held the position of Chief of the People's Commissariat of Internal Affairs, and was responsible together with Stalin for the brutal repression of 1938. By the end of that year, Stalin underwent a change of attitude with regard to the way in which "abuse of power" was defined. Stalin abdicated all responsibility, leaving the blame to be pointed at Yezhov, who was then removed from his position and a dossier against him was assembled; he was arrested in April 1939 and executed the following year (Victor, 2004, p. 369).

The Manichaeistic contention that "anyone who is not with me, is against me", as a form of controlling any kind of criticism, is always present in totalitarian regimes and creates deep social fragmentation and dissociation. Wang Shiwei, for instance, a young journalist during Mao's regime and an active member of the Communist Party, dared to openly express some critical views on issues he considered unfair. Sometime later, because Mao was unable to confront the truth of these allegations, he accused Shiwei of being a Trotskyist, ordered him to be imprisoned, tortured, and, sometime later, "hacked to death, and thrown into a dry well. He was forty-one" (Chang & Halliday, 2005, p. 243).

In 1936 Mao asked the Shanghai underground to find an American journalist who could sell his communist movement to the world. He contracted Edgar Snow who wrote for the *Saturday Evening Post*. Mao asked that Snow be provided with "security, secrecy, warmth and red carpet" (ibid., p. 192). He also checked everything he wrote, amending and rewriting parts, something Snow complained about in a letter to his wife, although it was never mentioned in the 1937 English-language publication of his book, *Red Star Over China*. Instead, he stated that Mao "never imposed any censorship on me" and that he had found Mao "honest and true". The book "played a big role in swaying Western opinion in favour of Mao" (ibid.).

We have been left wondering how such a cultivated country as Germany, capable of producing the greatest philosophical schools of thought, could have become such a focus of odium and a centre of destruction under the rule of Adolf Hitler and the Nazi party. How could they have produced the horrors of the concentration camps, the destruction of Judaism, and the ludicrous grandiosity in the belief of the Aryan ideal? Followers or acolytes are people capable of continuously complying with the leader's desires, never questioning, and, even worse, being absolutely destitute of inventiveness. They must be constantly well-informed about the leader's precise point of view on any subject in order to repeat verbatim whatever he has stated, and, most importantly, always be in terror of misinterpretation.

What drives these individuals to become unconditional followers of a given dictator? Bion (1948) described the three different matrixes of behaviour universally present in any "working" group, which he called "basic assumptions": a) "dependence", a group based on the need for protection, where people relate to their leader similarly to way in which children depend on parents; b) "pairing", meaning a group founded on "hope", similar to the idea present in the myth of the Virgin Mary and the birth of Christ, where a "couple" will produce a "Being" capable of gratifying all unfulfilled needs in the form of a true Messiah; in other words, there is the use of mechanisms of idealisation as a defence against hopelessness and depression to build the fantasy of a saviour and hero who will be rescued from ignominy and from being ignored, and ultimately will be revenged; c) "fight-flight", a group structured around "aggression" of attack and hiding. I believe these three forms of basic assumptions are always present and in use in totalitarian regimes. There can be other reasons, perhaps the most reasonable of which might related to what Winnicott (1960) has referred to as "false self personality". This trait can often be associated with other matters, such as: i) the need to be connected with someone who is idealised, because that person has been able to bring into practice fantasies shared with the individual but which the individual fears to act out; ii) themselves becoming "little dictators" and being able to exercise their quota of tyrannical power towards those under them; iii) the need to experience a sense of importance in order to conceal an inner sense of insignificance; iv) all of the above.

Donald Winnicott described the "false self" personality, a sort of "double face" or hypocrite, who will continuously comply with the powerful but at the same time derides the weaker; a kind of personality structure that fits well with military idiosyncrasy, where there is an analogous dynamic of blind obedience to the higher rank and an unrestrained demand placed on the subordinate. Acolytes are, most of the time, recruited from this group of individuals who lack backbone and are always willing to accommodate the dictator's demands. In a recent television programme portraying the endless monologues of the head of a totalitarian regime, the following exchange took place:

> X (the Dictator): "Human beings have been on the earth around
> 1500 years, eh François?"
> (He addresses someone in the crowd)
> "Well, a bit more," answers François very seriously.
> "What? 2000 then?" states X.

A comedian commenting on this dialogue, remarked:

> Obviously X is a total ignorant, because he doesn't know that if that were to be true the Greeks will be left out, and if it were even 2000 years the Egyptians, Sumerians and so on were not considered. Because François is a scientist he knows the truth that all of the statements made by the Dictator are absolute nonsense; but he must pay for his need to be there, to be part of such embarrassing stupidity, because his emotional need had induced him to be part of the circus.

Tyrants require followers either for the purposes of flattery, or for protection, to cover up wrongdoing. In order to keep them to hand, a high level of corruption is required, in the form of special privileges or financial and political power. Victor (1998) states:

> When the extent of his regime's destructiveness was revealed, Nazis defended him, saying Hitler did not initiate or even know about the worst. They argued that Goebbels, Göring, Himmler, or Bormann were mainly responsible and had manipulated Hitler. The evidence against that conclusion is overwhelming. The outline of the destructiveness to come was already in Hitler's mind when he wrote *Mein Kampf* in 1924, before Goebbels and the others played their parts. The motives—the craving for revenge, for war, and for extermination of Jews—were Hitler's. (p. 7)

CHAPTER SIX

Sycophants and socialist romantics

Truth might get ill, but never dies.

—Miguel de Cervantes

I will not be silent, even if your finger, just touching the mouth or the temple, heralds silence or threatens fear. Is there not a noble spirit? Shall we always feel what we said, but never said what we feel?[1]

—Francisco de Quevedo

Altogether, totalitarian regimes have been responsible for millions of deaths; the five dictators I will be considering in this study, according to various reports, amount to the astonishing number of 178,310,000 deaths; distributed as follows:

Mao:	70,000,000
Hitler:	65,000,000
Stalin:	43,000,000
Hussein:	300,000
Castro:	10,000
Total:	**178,310,000**

45

That, clearly, is a considerable number of dead, an expression of violence carried to extremes, as well as a message to those who, "naively", have convinced themselves that totalitarian leaders can ever be guided by humanitarian purposes, rather than understanding that in fact they are driven by selfish desire and belief and the completely disregard of the lives and needs of individuals.

I describe as "romantics" those individuals, usually well-known writers, journalists, philosophers, professionals, and so on, who through their work support totalitarian dictators, although always stay within the comfort of their own countries, away from the suffering of those who are directly exposed to and forced to deal with the dictators' immediate range of power and arbitrary action, often deprived of their freedom to make choices or decisions, who are persecuted, threatened, and often killed. Perhaps "romantics" might not be the most appropriate label, because these individuals are always driven, similarly to totalitarian dictators, by unconscious childhood needs relating to ambivalence about authority figures, problems of sexual identity, sometimes in the form of latent homosexuality, where the concern for the suffering people, if any, is secondary. They identify with totalitarian dictators because they share the same unconscious fantasies, but lack the intensity and aggressive boldness of the tyrant, having, consequently, a sort of unconscious homosexual surrender to the power of an aggressive father. These individuals, however, can become immensely dangerous, because due to their own personal achievements—some are even Nobel Prize winners—they are well-known, considered serious, honest, and well-esteemed worldwide.

Marx and Engels

The first romantic socialists to make important theoretical contributions were Karl Marx and Friedrich Engels. According to them, "social history" is a record of past struggles between the bourgeoisie, or those who had land, resources, factories, and other means of production, and the proletariat, who worked for wages and had little. In its efforts to be successful, the bourgeoisie has persistently adjusted and transformed the means of production, guaranteeing a steady infusion of capital by creating larger cities and promoting new and cheaper commodities. As capital and the production of the bourgeoisie increases, the labour of the proletariat not only becomes less valuable, but also alienates them from themselves, from each other, and from the commodities they help to produce. Workers have little influence over the politics of change and production; and even small shopkeepers and trained labourers are encouraged to join with the bourgeoisie in its drive for capital, instead of defending their logical association with wage earners.

According to Marx and Engels, the proletariat represents not only the mainstream of the population, but also the hope for an efficient political accomplishment that will eventually increase the presence of communism in the world. "Marx," said Popper (1971) "made an honest attempt to apply rational methods to the most urgent problems of social life" (p. 81). "He had a burning desire to help the oppressed, and was fully conscious of the need for proving himself in deeds and not only in words" (ibid., p. 82). Marx was such an honest person and a product of 1800s "Romanticism" that, unlike many other philosophers, he lived precisely as he preached: he and his family lived on the charity of friends and died in absolute poverty. Marx was the first and the greatest of all romantics.

In spite of his merits, continues Popper,

> Marx was, I believe, a false prophet. He was a prophet of the course of history, and his prophecies did, not come true … he misled scores of intelligent people [and others not so intelligent!] into believing that historical prophecy is the scientific way of approaching social problems. (Ibid., p. 82)

It is quite obvious that for a country such as Russia, after hundreds of years under the domination of rogue and merciless monarchies, communism was the right solution; even more so if the changes were to be effected by someone like Lenin, and nobody foresaw at that point the forthcoming pathological sadism of Stalin. We can always wonder what would have happened if over one hundred years previously, in 1812, Napoleon had succeeded in bringing the French Revolution to Russia.

Sartre and Beauvoir

Jean-Paul Sartre, the French philosopher, together with his companion Simone de Beauvoir, can be considered two of the romantic supporters of totalitarianism. Sartre described himself as a communist, although his politics frequently appeared rather incoherent and contradictory.

According to Simone de Beauvoir, Sartre was motivated not by loy-
alty and devotion to the Party, but by his own personal negativistic
attitude about social privileges that Beauvoir once declared a total
"anti-bourgeois anarchism"; or, as he stated, the bourgeoisie induced in
him "a hatred that could only die with me" (Kolakowski, 1985). Respond-
ing to his own internal call and induced by his existential approach to
the "human side" of individuals, Sartre imagined himself a bourgeoisie
and in order to compensate resorted to becoming a full member of the
French Communist Party. He attempted to reconcile communism and
existentialism in his *Critique of Dialectical Reason*, and, later, in his unfin-
ished biography of Flaubert, he tried psychoanalysis too. He started
the left-wing newspaper *Libération*, and together with Beauvoir, took
up Maoism and was arrested for selling the forbidden Maoist paper
La cause du people on the streets. He even ended his friendship with
Camus after Camus accused him of totalitarianism. He later became
seriously involved in a political movement against the Vietnam War,
and in 1967 headed the International War Crimes Tribunal organised by
Bertrand Russell to consider American military conduct in Indochina.
Among the New Left, Sartre was highly recognised, and his position
on French colonial policy in Algeria became widely known. Sometime
later, in the early 1960s, the Cuban economic and social "revolution"
fascinated Sartre to the point that he met Fidel Castro, but broke off
with him after he became a dictator. Raffy (2004), who gave an account
of this visit, suggested that perhaps not only did the topic affect the
judgement of the French, but Castro also managed to bewitch them:
"Later in France, Sartre wrote to the journal *France-Soir* a series of arti-
cles appropriate for a first communion child. He had seen nothing of
the Island but felt they had visited it from side to side" (p. 375). Castro,
who imposed something of a marathon on Sartre and Beauvoir, accompanied them everywhere. Sartre was stunned by the impressive figure
of the revolutionary man, stating that "he could never be defeated".
One day Fidel invited Sartre to have lemonade by the beach, but when
the waiter served the drink, it was warm. Castro called the boy and got
him to find a cold one. "Sartre was astonished" that such a leader of
the Third World "could have become as concerned with the temperature of a glass of lemonade, as for strategic predicaments. Was not that
marvellous?" In the face of Castro, Sartre was "like a naïve child who
swallowed anything. But this was not unique. Fidel enthralled dozens of
intellectuals whom he considered absolute cretins" (ibid., pp. 375–376).

Sartre became a total flatterer of the leader, and later remembered an "extraordinary" conversation he had with him:

> "All men had the right for what they ask," Castro told me.
> "And if they were to ask for the moon?" I asked.
> He grabbed his cigar, saw that it was still lighted, put it aside and turned towards me.
> "If they ask for the moon, it is because they need it."

And Sartre concluded, dazzled by so much profundity:

> "I have few friends because I give too much importance to friend-ship. After this answer I understood that Castro has become one of them." However, the author of *Being and Nothingness* later discov-ered that Fidel Castro never had any friends. (Ibid., p. 376)

The interpreter Juan Arocha remembered afterwards the infantile joy Castro experienced from manipulating those "great monuments of the European intelligentsia". "Castro never liked either culture or intellec-tuals" (ibid., p. 375).

In 1955, Sartre and de Beauvoir travelled to China to visit Mao Tse-tung and decided to write a book about the country and to praise Mao's revolutionary violence as "profoundly moral", while de Beauvoir compared him to Roosevelt. In their book on Mao, Chang and Halliday (2005) have this to say about that visit:

> Mao could easily pull the wool over most visitors' eyes. When the French writer Simone de Beauvoir visited in 1955, even the French-speaking Chinese woman assigned to accompany her had to get special permission to speak to her directly without going through the interpreter. After her short visit, de Beauvoir pontificated that "the power he [Mao] exercises is no more dictatorial than, for exam-ple Roosevelt's was." New China's Constitution renders impossible the concentration of authority in one man's hand ... Mao made sure that no Chinese except a very carefully vetted elite could get out of the country. (p. 460)

Mao managed to deceive people about what was going on in China, about the famine, executions, dictatorial power, and so on. In this group of "romantic apologists" of Mao were also French François Mitterrand; Canadian Pierre Trudeau, who co-wrote a book about China; British Field Marshal Montgomery; and Harvard professor John K. Fairbank, who, after returning from China, stated that the "Maoist revolution was the best thing that happened to Chinese peoples in centuries" (ibid.). "The brutal truth," said Ranold Radosh (2005):

> ... to put it as starkly as possible, is that Mao Tse-tung was the last century's most violent and vicious ruler—a power mad figure *who dreamt of extending his rule to the entire world*, a goal he pursued while engaging in murder, torture, rape and forced starvation, while demanding complete obedience to his every whim, all the while attended by personal servants who offered him every luxury he desired. (Ibid., my emphasis)

García Marquez

At present, Fidel Castro, one of the most relevant dictators with the longest period in power, also possesses his own circle of flatterers, or well-known individuals willing to write panegyrics, similar to those published about other preceding autocrats. Colombian Nobel Prize-winner García Marquez (2006), who lived for some time in Cuba, very recently wrote an acclamation on the occasion of Castro's withdrawal from power prior to a major surgical intervention. From the two pages of continuous idealisation of Castro written by García Marquez, we have chosen at random just one out of fifteen other paragraphs written with the sole purpose of eulogising Castro:

> When he [Castro] speaks to people in the street ... they address him as Fidel. They surround him without any fear, they argue, contradict, complain, in a close communication where truth circulates copiously. It is then when the unwanted human being is discovered, who has been concealed by the radiance of his own image. This is the Fidel Castro I know: a man of austere habits and insatiable illusions with an old fashioned formal education, of cautious words and soft manners, unable to conceive any idea unless it is colossal. (p. 2)

We do not deny that what has been expressed here is true, we only submit that it must represent only half of the truth; if not, then ask the relatives of those who have been jailed or assassinated, or those who have lost their lives in attempting to escape from their own country, or those forced to live in exile who have lost everything, or whatever is left of the opposition in Cuba, a nation without free elections, run in anger and revenge by a "family" who have declared themselves absolute owners and rulers.

We will now recount an incident portrayed in *Castro, el desleal* (Castro, the Unfaithful)[2] (2004), a book by Serge Raffy, a French journalist who spent time in Cuba. He is describing the consequences of a terrible famine experienced on the island at the beginning of the nineties, considered by many a direct result of the politic carried out by Castro and the Communist government:

> With a greater frequency they were facing him [Castro] in public. During one meeting with Health Minister Hector Terry, specialist in epidemiology and one of the few black ministers in the government, Castro complained about the serious outbreak of polyneuritis affecting over 50.000 Cubans, mostly children. Castro blamed the politic about hygiene carried out by the Health Ministry, and Terry calmly answered, that the only one responsible for such an epidemic was the lack of food that was affecting the whole country. The Maximum Leader, feeling accused, was infuriated, lost control, and started to scream as if he was possessed until he suddenly felt suffocated. All of a sudden he was quiet, paralysed and unable to utter any word. His Minister's insolence had provoked a terrible paroxysm. His bodyguards rushed towards him and took him out in a hurry. Some days later, Hector Terry was fired without any explanation. He had committed the crime of stating the truth about the drama of the polyneuritis ... (p. 534)

If García Marquez felt the way he wrote, how come he was living—like Sartre in France—in "free Colombia" instead of Cuba? Why do "romantic socialists" produce this type of panegyric about totalitarian leaders? Is it because they truly ignore what remains unsaid? Shall we say like Dante: "There is a special place in Hell for those who remain silent"? However, in the cases we are referring to now, it is worse than remaining silent, because these romantic sycophants are doing all they can to hide the truth.

For Esteban and Panichelli (2004), what brought García Marquez close to Castro was a hunger for power that went beyond his literary interests, the need to reach, at any price, an emotional closeness with those in the uppermost political positions, to the point that in spite of widely publicised information, he denies the torture, killing, and extreme human rights abuses that systematically take place in Cuba. According to the authors, García Marquez depicts the island as a utopian paradise where "there is not a single human being without shoes, a home, without his three daily meals … he has either allowed his passion to blind his understanding of the island, or chosen to display submission to those who control the power in Cuba." Castro on the other hand, is thrilled to use a Nobel Prize-awarded writer as an unofficial ambassador of the Cuban revolution. In 1982, Castro provided García Marquez with a mansion in the best neighbourhood of Havana as well as a Mercedes with chauffeur for his exclusive use at a time when housing and cars were extremely scarce commodities in Cuba (p. 204).

Neruda

In his poem "The Grapes and the Wind," Neruda (1954) presents a ghastly and unnerving acclamation of Stalin:

> We must learn from Stalin
> He entered History in the company of Lenin and the wind …
> Stalin is the noon,
> The maturity of man and the people …
> His sincere intensity
> His concrete clarity …
> Stalinist workers, clerics, women take care of this day!
> The light has not vanished
> The fire has not disappeared,
> There is the only growth of
> Like, bread, fire and hope
> In Stalin's invisible time! …
> In recent years the dove,
> Peace, the wandering persecuted rose
> Found herself on his shoulders

Those who did not think like him, Neruda accused of being followers of Franco, a bunch of "sons of bitches, silent accomplices of the executioner". "Neruda," answered Juan Ramón Jiménez, "is a great lousy poet."

Cuba was also present in Neruda's muse, and he wrote a book titled *Canción de gesta*, which was a literary form that flourished in France during the eleventh century. Published in 1960, it was the first text ever written by a well-known author in support of the Cuban revolution; however, from the very beginning, Castro developed a dislike of Neruda and his work. When they met personally for the first time in 1972 at the Cuban embassy in Caracas—Neruda later remembered in his *Memoirs*—a photographer, who became aware of the presence of the two men, took a picture using a flash that attracted the attention of Castro who then lost control, grabbed the photographer by the neck, took away his camera, and threw him out of the room. "Why did he reject the picture so rambunctiously?" asked Neruda. "Perhaps because he did not wish to see himself in a picture with a pro-Soviet poet." Others speculated that some aspects of *Canción de gesta* were not well accepted, such as the part dedicated to Fidel, where the cult of the individual is made less of in favour of the collective. There was another issue. In 1966 Neruda was invited to the USA by his friend Arthur Miller during an international encounter at the PEN congress in New York, where he read his poem "Violently anti-imperialist". In July of that same year, the Cuban paper *Granma* published a long open letter to Neruda, signed by several Cuban intellectuals, where he was accused of weakness and complacency about the "enemy imperialist".

Heidegger

Shortly after Hitler seized power, Heidegger, the existential German philosopher, joined the Nazi party, becoming rector of the University of Freiburg in May 1933, where he read his infamous inaugural address, inducing students and faculty members to serve the Nazi government. It seems as if his main ambition was to become the "philosopher" of Hitler's regime. In another speech, delivered in June of the same year to the Heidelberg Student Association, he referred to the position that universities should take according to the new Nazi order. He stated:

> University study must again become a risk, not a refuge for the cowardly. Whoever does not survive the battle, lies where he falls. The new courage must accustom itself to steadfastness, for the battle for the institutions where our leaders are educated will continue for a long time. It will be fought out of the strengths of the new

> Reich that Chancellor Hitler will bring to reality. A hard race with
> no thought of self must fight this battle, a race that lives from con-
> stant testing and that remains directed toward the goal to which
> it has committed itself. It is a battle to determine who shall be the
> teachers and leaders at the university. (Wolin, 1992, p. 45)

In October 1933, Hitler declared himself *Führer* and Heidegger was elected university *Führer-Rector* with absolute power similar to Hitler's position over Germany. A month later, he issued a decree whereby the Nazi position on racial supremacy was to be applied to the university students, where economic aid was to be given to students belonging to the SS, the SA, and other military groups, but was to be denied to anyone considered non-Aryan according to Nazi law. By the end of that same year, he requested financial aid to write a book of Hitler's speeches to be distributed around the world, adding to his request a note stating that "Needless to say, non-Aryans shall not appear on the signature page" (ibid.). There is a long history of Heidegger being an informant to the Nazi authorities of students and colleagues, moti-vated by racism or intolerance of different political creeds, as was the case with Hermann Staudinger, Eduard Baumgarten, and Max Müller, who all lost their jobs as university professors. There is particularly the issue of Heidegger's treatment of his former teacher, Edmund Husserl, founder of the philosophical school of phenomenology, who had an international reputation equal to that of Heidegger, who was denied use of the university library at Freiburg because he was a Jew. There was no other reason, besides anti-Semitism, why his mentor Husserl's original dedication was removed from the 1945 edition of his master-piece *Sein und Zeit*. After the war, Heidegger did not write a disclaimer of Nazism, in spite of the fact that some of his friends, such as Karl Jasper and Herbert Marcuse, advised him to do so, to repudiate crimes committed during Hitler's regime.

CHAPTER SEVEN

The claustrum

The problem we are facing in relation to this chapter is that the meaning of what we wish to express now might be better understood by two extremes of social stratum: either the rough and vulgar or the very sophisticated; a middle echelon, representing the main level we are trying to reach with this book, can be left out.

Vulgar and colloquial communication is often rejected not only because of its closeness to the truth, but also because it is broadcast in such an open, primitive, and violent form that it can be experienced by many as too disgusting, a sort of desecration. Take, for instance, the crude but common expression (the scripts in any of Hollywood's violent movies is completely saturated with it) of "mother fucker". The two extreme strata I have referred to above might also grasp the power of such expression: the intuitive, unsophisticated, vulgar, common people who, with a purpose in mind, originally created it; or Sigmund Freud who explained its unconscious meaning. Incestuous relationship with the mother is such an unparalleled and sordid act that it is extremely uncommon in practice. Why then, if it is so unusual, has such an expression been chosen as the utmost degrading insult? The understanding of this contradiction was provided by Freud, who discovered that there was a universal desire in every child for special love and attention, together with the child's own sexual fantasies—which are different from the adult's—towards the parent of the opposite sex; something that now is common knowledge and that Freud depicted as the "Oedipus complex". It is this desire, which all males harbour deep inside their unconscious towards their mother, that provides the expression "mother fucker" with its insulting power. Now, how can the people who have never read Freud find out about the power implicit in such an expression?[1]

Donald Meltzer (1992), a British psychoanalyst, referred to metaphorical spaces or *claustrum* pertaining to the mother's body, where individuals can figuratively remain "mentally confined". These are important mental constructions relating to psychological attitudes, which, of course, cannot be understood in a literary manner. We should not be surprised, as we have stated elsewhere in this book, that from the moment we are conceived inside our mother's body, we are no different from any of her internal organs. In this sense, the uterus is an organ ruled by the exactness of time and space: by the end of around thirty-six weeks (time), we will be expelled into the external world, as a different and biologically autonomous individual[2] (space). However, there remains in the unconscious vestiges of this experience, as a desire to return to the "protection" of the womb, or to regress, depend on, or to become fused with our mother's desire. Dependency is a feeling all human beings are unconsciously fated to entertain, as a direct consequence of those sheltered years of childhood. There is, however, at the same time, the horror of becoming aware of this dependency. Congruent with these unconscious desires to regress, there can also be similar desires on the part of the parents, mostly the mother, that their children remain as such forever, something depicted by the Greek myth of Pan.

The anus, on the other hand, different from the uterus, represents an organ related to feelings of "control" and "retention", characteristics originating directly from the early years of "anal education". Socialisation is a process requiring absolute domestication of all anal manifestations and its derivatives; however, this demand can easily turn into a battle between parents and children, because the latter may find toilet training extremely confusing. Toddlers, who have no feeling of disgust toward their faeces and sometimes can even eat them, sense their parents' interest to deposit them in a special place, such as the potty, as proof that what they have "'produced" constitutes an extremely valuable "gift"! It is very difficult for children to understand that what the parents have demanded of them with such emphasis, to the point that they can react with extreme rage if it is not properly

endorsed, is about something absolutely disgusting that must be immediately flushed away. Such a contradiction represents a narcissistic blow
that can, when not properly handled, induce all sorts of symptoms that
usually condense in what Freud referred to as "anal character".

Using Freud's concepts of the "infantile phases of sexual development", known as "oral", "anal", and "genital", Meltzer (1992) described
three regressive "maternal spaces" or *claustrum*: a) head/breast,
b) genital, and c) maternal rectum. The head/breast can be represented
by the attitude or behaviour present in a person or a culture often associated with "richness":

> ... at first concrete and related to urgent need of nourishment,
> becomes diversified in its nuances: generosity, receptiveness,
> aesthetic reciprocity. (Meltzer, 1992, p. 72)

When seen from inside, says Meltzer,

> ... generosity becomes *quid pro quo*, receptiveness becomes invei-
> glement, reciprocity becomes collusion, understanding becomes
> penetration of secrets, knowledge becomes information, symbol
> formation becomes metonymy, art becomes fashion. (pp. 72–73)

Of the second space, or genital claustrum, Meltzer described the following characteristics:

> The inmates of this space are more obviously disturbed and
> turbulent ... they live in a space that is dominated by a primitive
> "priapic" religion. (Ibid., p. 88)
> ... seen from the interior is Mardi Gras ... for the essence of this
> interior view is that the entry of the father's phallus is celebrated
> and enjoyed voluptuously by all the babies, while the mother
> calmly receives this homage. (Ibid., p. 89)

In the third space or maternal rectum "we are essentially", says
Meltzer:

> ... in the world of addiction, where the individual has consigned
> his survival to the mercy of a malignant object. (Ibid., p. 92)

We will now refer to the space we consider most relevant to the nature of
our present work. The main issue here is the idealisation of faeces, where

the child becomes the mother's fantasy of an envious and revengeful internal anal object. By projecting this internal object into him, she can shape him into something we have previously described using the symbolism of the "faecal phallus" (López-Corvo, 1993). This is a mechanism more often found in boys than girls, and represents the image of someone so important for his mother that she overprotects him to the point of rendering him completely useless. He is the mother's unconscious (hidden) phallus, who at the same time is also a total failure. Remembering Freud's statement of "penis = faeces = baby", the oedipal "child–faecal–phallus" is eternally hidden in his mother's rectum where he will remain motionless as a dead object. Dictators can usually be placed within this space. When there is, in addition, a very aggressive father who unfairly threatens the mother and her son, the boy will grow up feeling that he must rescue his mother from the threat of that terrible injustice.

Inside the dictator's claustrum

There is a significant presence of anal traits in the characters of dictators, such as the strong need to possess, control, and enviously destroy, or the narcissistic desire to be admired or well thought of, as a form of compensation for not feeling good about themselves, debased, like nothing, like faeces. These feelings result from early and serious forms of ill-treatment, of being continuously desecrated and castrated by aggressive fathers, with no one to turn to. Children in this condition will later on desperately try to exercise some form of control, to feel, as compensation, that they are now in command, and to treat others like dirt, nothing, or faeces, as a form of revenge. At the same time there has also been a secret idealisation of this child by the mother, who identifies him as her saviour; or, in Freud's terminology, as her unconscious phallus. Feeling a dweller in the maternal claustrum is a natural process for the future dictator who will later place a whole nation in his own claustrum, discriminating, in Manichean fashion, between those who comply and those who rebel. Such contrasts in the process of identification, resulting from the combination of serious castration threats from a violent father and the secret idealisation from a dependent mother, can unconsciously structure, in the mind of the future dictator, the image of a faecal phallus, where he feels that he is everything and, at the same time, nothing. In the cases of children who have been idealised by dependent mothers, but whose father has been absent, the result is addictive behaviour.

CHAPTER EIGHT

Unconditionality, essentiality, and revengeful hope

When there is no Justice, it is dangerous to be right.
—Francisco de Quevedo

"Unconditional love" and the confusion of the animate with the inanimate

We have previously stated that, since babies are formed inside the mother's body, they remain for some time undifferentiated from any of her internal organs. In other words, at the very beginning of our lives, we are literally another appendage of our mother's body. After birth, the child moves into natural symbiotic dependency with the mother, similar to an inanimate object or some kind of commodity; until, progressively, the child is rescued from the status of "commodity" to that of "human being", by the active and loving presence of the father. There is in psychoanalysis the expression that "the phallus introduces the symbol", meaning that fathers allow children to move away from their dependency on their mothers by means of abstract thinking and, eventually, freedom and autonomy. Because men are mentally, physiologically, and anatomically different from women, they lack the mental capacity to supply children with their biological needs, as mothers do. In other words, fathers provide freedom and hope, while the mother provides the essentials: life and unconditional love.

Symbolisation is a crucial mechanism that brings about mental growth, and consists, in general terms, in the aptitude to replace concrete thinking with abstract mental representations, something that takes place normally in the formation of language. For instance, there is a common agreement in any English-speaking individual that the word "book" stands for that specific object we use and like to read. The word itself has no specific attachment to the object that it represents, but there is a consensus that such a word is a legitimate representation of that particular object. Adults are capable of remaining calm while away from those they love because, thanks to their mental representation, they know where the loved one is and that they are well, different from little children who constantly "feed" on the physical presence of their mothers in order to remain calm. This interaction, between the child and the mother's presence or absence, has given rise to an aspect of psychology known as "separation anxiety".

There are two other extremely important natural circumstances, which are usually unnoticed, that act on the character of a child, and of the parents, and help children mentally to move towards a further sense of trust and independency, to achieve a state of "selfness", and differentiation between inanimate things and animate beings. We are referring to what it is known as the "refusing no" or the "terrible twos", and a bit later, the "temper tantrums".

The refusing no or obstinate negativism that two-year-old children all over the world always display, represents nature saying, through the child, "I am here", or "I am different from you". For instance, if you raise your hand and then suddenly drop it, the air that your hand meets on the way down will say "yes", but if you meet a table, for instance, as your hand falls, the table in your way will say "no, I am here". Negativism, in other words, is a way in which nature reveals, and provides, a sense of presence and identity to human beings. Temper tantrums, on the other hand, represent a crucial test of parents' infinite endurance; if they "pass" such a test and provide "unlimited patience", such an attitude will create in children an inner sense of being loved unconditionally, of being loved for what they "are" and not for what they "do" or "have". Physical punishment carries with it terrible risks and complications, inducing a deep sense of helplessness and terror that later translates into clinical depression, low self-esteem, destructive aggression, and even suicide.

Unconditional love is the main source of inner feelings of well-being and hope; it is what differentiates humans from things or commodities. Things or inanimate objects have worth according to their extrinsic value: a chair, for instance, will be preserved depending on its price or on the particular affects that have been projected onto it, and usually a chair that is broken and worthless will not be kept; however, a sensible person will not usually throw away his or her grandmother because she is old and useless. When we feel—either consciously or unconsciously—that we are loved for what we *do* or *have* and not for what we *are*, we are definitely confusing ourselves with a thing, with an inanimate object. This condition is a constant and appalling source of suffering and anxiety. To feel loved for what we do and not for what we are creates an unconscious dependency on other people's judgement, on what they say, whether good or bad, disregarding the fact that in reality we always remain the same, in spite of what others think or say about us. After all, truth does not need a thinker; the sky is blue by itself. Also, and very importantly, violence is at the heart of such confusion, in the sense that it is extremely difficult, if not impossible, to produce harm when there is an insightful perception of aliveness about ourselves as well as about others. It is easier to destroy a "thing" than to destroy a "life". The brutal and senseless killing we witness in the news every day is most of the time the product of a failure to distinguish the animate from the inanimate. If the tiger were to be aware of the suffering of the gazelle, it would starve to death. At the core of senseless violence there is always the confusion between the animate and the inanimate, between being human and being a thing.

"Essentiality"

The fact that babies, for nine months, constitute an internal organ of the mother induces in her a powerful sense of possession that is usually referred to as the "natural maternal symbiosis". In certain situations, such as with adolescent mothers or women who, as children have been emotionally deprived or who have experienced a sense of having little or nothing, children can be treated as if they are a possession of the mother, like a doll. Such an attitude eventually induces in the child an unconscious sense of essentiality or indispensability, in that he or she becomes absolutely central to the mother's ability to achieve any sense of well-being. This is because cultures around the world are still, in many ways, very phallocentric; boys are usually chosen over girls to become the mother's rescuer or saviour.

There is a Dutch story, "The boy who held back the sea", that sketches out this sense of essentiality:

> Jan found, by chance, that the mighty ocean was leaking through a small hole in the city's dyke. Even a naughty boy like Jan knew that a small leak unchecked would get bigger and that if the dyke should give way a terrible flood would drown the whole town … He wrapped a handkerchief around his finger and dug it into the tiny gap in the earthen wall … for now, at least the flow stopped … When the people discovered what he had done, the town held a great festival to honour the young hero who had saved everybody from the worst flood since Noah.

It is obvious that this story contains a sense of mockery about little Jan claiming that he held the mighty sea from flooding a whole town just by placing his finger in the tiny hole in the dyke. But this is exactly what a child feels who has been made to believe that he is indispensable to fulfilling his mother's real and "mighty" needs. That a helpless little child can successfully look after his adult parent is a senseless belief and can result, eventually, in a common and serious psychopathology that we could describe as a kind of "pseudo-adultisation". Since becoming the parents' rescuers is impossible, the child will always develop two different emotions: i) he will grow up with serious emotional ambivalence, meaning that on one hand he will feel compelled to initiate, and participate in, noteworthy enterprises, while at the same time experiencing an inner feeling of failure, resulting, finally in total paralysis; it can be summarised as follows: "How to do everything in order to do nothing"; ii) because the mother always needs to be able to pay attention to other children or to the father, the child will always experience a sense of being excluded or left out, which will induce the feeling that, since he has not been the one chosen, someone else is satisfying his mother's needs and desires. This fantasy will automatically increase rivalry against the father and other siblings, as well as omnipotent feelings—as in the story of little Jan—that he should be his mother's true and absolute saviour. There are, however other conditions that, when present, will make this form of "basic delusion" even more powerful; for instance, as we have mentioned before, a mother who has significant needs to be rescued, together with the loss of previous siblings and the presence of a real threat from an aggressive and terrorising husband. Such conditions are often present in the histories of totalitarian dictators such as Stalin, Hitler, Hussein, and Castro.

"Basic delusion"

This form of interaction between the mother and the child can be referred to as the "basic delusion" (López-Corvo, 2003). Freud proposed that for all women there is an unconscious formula of baby = penis, implying that there is a narcissistic identification between babies—mostly boys— and women's unconscious compensation for the absence of a phallus. In other words, women feel unconsciously that giving birth to a son will fulfil the long-standing desire to achieve some of the characteristics they have idealised in men: "now they have produced their own penis". We are not implying that men are in any way better than women; rather that biological and social conditions superficially create the appearance that men are biologically better endowed and have more privileges than women. The fact, for instance, that reproduction relies mostly on women's biology, will usually demand more responsibility and com- mitment from women than from men; in this sense, the practicalities of reproduction and child rearing can create the mistaken impression that women are more committed and men have more freedom. Men can also give the impression of being physically stronger than women, better able to perform certain tasks, and so on. We believe that what is greater than women's phallic envy is the more concealed envy in men of women's ability to produce life. All major religions rely basically on this form of envy of men towards women; it is sufficient to read what any of the existing "sacred books" say about women. One of us has presented this view in a book: *The Women Within* (López-Corvo, 2009).

Feelings of indispensability are logical and even necessary in order to sustain the natural symbiosis between mother and child. But these feelings will be increased to pathological levels when the mother, attempting to resolve her own dependency, resorts to using a particular child to unconsciously "complete herself", and to use this relation- ship to deny her feelings of dependency and convince herself that she needs no one. The "basic delusion" represents a fantasy, a belief that the mother requires the child in order to survive, but in reality this feeling is not real. This concept is important because later on, when she acts out her own needs or pre-conceptual traumas, she will repeat exactly the same feelings she experienced as a child. A child might be chosen by his mother depending on any number of characteristics; however, in the particular cases we are now researching, there are certain conditions that increase the sense of unconditionality: 1) the deaths of previous children, 2) violent fathers, and 3) young, uneducated, and dependent mothers. We have found that these conditions are very much present in the early years of those dictators we have investigated in this book.

Revengeful hope

As we have stated previously, there exists, on the part of children, a "basic delusion", or the feeling that they are absolutely indispensable to their mothers' ability to achieve a state of well-being. However, children soon find out that there are other members in the household whom their mothers also rely on and pay attention to, primarily the father or whoever takes his place, as well as other children, mostly those who have been born later. Basic delusion is just that—a delusion or make-believe experienced by children when they realise that they are not the mother's narcissistic completion of a state of well-being, or, in other words, are not the narcissistic replacement of the absent phallus. However, since they believe that the mother needs someone to complete this "basic fault", they produce the fantasy that someone else is doing it. It is a fantasy that also induces rivalry, envy, and a need for revenge or, better, a "revengeful hope", because children feel that if they were able to get rid of their supposed rival, they would fulfil the *hope* of becoming the ones who totally complete their mothers' absences. This means that the fantasy is guided by a powerful feeling of revenge, a revenge believed by the person to be the only hope, as an all-or-nothing solution to their continuous suffering. Later in their lives these individuals might find the means to exercise this unconscious revenge, such as any form of power—money, politics, delinquency, and so on. Perhaps in totalitarians there is an inability to be creative and out of frustration they resort to political power in order to exercise revenge, while creative people resort to art and to making things to unconsciously do the same. In summary, there are three main things to consider: a) feelings of indispensability or the right to possess the mother, and later on the country; b) early childhood traumatic threat that involves physical aggression, mostly from the father; c) an excessive sense of self-envy and the destruction of creativity.

Freud used a different means of explaining these feelings of "revengeful hope", by discussing Shakespeare's Richard III, who suffered from a physical deformity that drove him to intrigue, murder, and frivolity:

> And therefore, since I cannot prove a lover,
> To entertain these fair well-spoken days,
> I am determinèd to prove a villain
> And hate the idle pleasures of these days.

"Richard," said Freud (1916d), "seems to say nothing more than":

> ... As I cannot play the lover on account of my deformity, I will play the villain ... I may do wrong myself, since wrong has been done to me ... Why did not Nature give us the ... noble profile of aristocracy? Why were we born in a middle-class home instead of in a royal palace? We could carry off beauty and distinction quite as well as any of those whom we are now obliged to envy for these qualities. (1916, pp. 313–314)

CHAPTER NINE

Hitler

"**B**y the time Adolf Hitler became Germany's leader," says Victor (1998, p. 21), "he was convinced he had been chosen supernaturally to save his nation in the world. His egocentrism and grandiosity began early in his childhood and grew until he saw himself as bold truly divine." Adolf Hitler was born in Braunau am Inn, a town in present-day Austria, on 20 April 1889. The son of Alois Hitler and Klara Polz, he was the fourth but eldest child of six, because his three older siblings—Gustav, Ida, and Otto—died in infancy, and a younger brother, Edmund, died from measles when Adolf was nine. Eventually there were only two children left—Adolf and Paula his youngest sister. There were two other children from his father's previous marriage: Alois Jr. and Angela.

Alois Hitler, Hitler's father, was the illegitimate son of Maria Schicklgruber, who became pregnant—supposedly—by Leopold Frankenberger, while working as a maid for a wealthy Jewish family. When Alois was five, Maria married George Hiedler, a union that lasted only a few months. After their separation, Alois went to live with Johann Nepomuk Hiedler, Maria's brother-in-law, a farmer in the town of Spital, considered better-off and more accountable than George. "Thus, Alois's first years were marked by neglect and loss," says Victor (1998):

His father, whoever he was, failed to acknowledge Alois as his
son. And before he was six, Alois also lost everyone he knew—his
mother, his godparents, his stepfather and whatever playmate he
had in Strones ... The cause of her [his mother's] death five years
later was given as tuberculosis ... She may already have been too
infirm to care for Alois ... Whatever the reason, he was too young
to understand why he lost her. (p. 14)

And also:

Alois lived with Nepomuk's family until he was thirteen, when
he left for Vienna to be apprenticed to a shoemaker ... He decided
to teach himself and learned enough by age eighteen to leave the
shoemaker's trade and enter the civil service, first as a border guard
and then in the Customs Service. (Ibid., p. 15)

At thirty-six he married Anna Glas–Horer, a wealthier woman fourteen
years his senior. When Anna became ill he brought his "niece", Klara
Polz, to look after her. She was Nepomuk's—Alois's adopted father—
granddaughter, who addressed him as "uncle". Alois, who was a sort
of "Don Juan", seduced Klara who was sixteen years old, as well as the
maid, Franziska Matzelsberger who was fourteen:

Perhaps the fact that he was having affairs ... under the roof he
shared with Anna was too much for her. Unable to divorce him, she
obtained a separation and moved away. (Ibid., p. 20)

After Anna's death Alois sent Klara away and married Franziska
with whom he had two children: Alois Jr. and Angela. Sometime later
Franziska fell ill and in order to care for her he sent for Klara again. By the
time of Franziska's death Klara was already pregnant. Because they were
relatives, to marry her required a special dispensation from the church.
Haunted by the stigma of illegitimacy, Alois had already acquired—when
he was forty—proof of legitimacy by producing witnesses who declared
that he was a true son of Nepomuk Hiedler, Klara's grandfather. It was a
legal arrangement conveniently made some time after Nepomuk's death.
Being completely destitute and facing a rather obscure future as a maid,
Klara, twenty-three years younger than Alois, choose to marry him; after
all, he had managed to achieve a prestigious position in the customs
service, rising to a rank equivalent to that of army captain.

By community standards, Alois was a success—a hard worker who supported his family, a solid citizen, and a person of prominence. (His drinking, affairs, roughness with his family hardly counted against him. That was what man did.) He had come a long way from being a penniless waif. (Ibid.)

His will to achieve was possibly an unconscious compensation for all that he lacked, such as not knowing who his father was, the suspicion that he was the descendent of a Jew, having to borrow a name that he, possibly ambivalently, misspelled. Alois was short in stature with a flat nose and a big head, bold as well as mean and disparaging. Klara, on the other hand, was tall and slim, easy-going, pleasant, and felt by many to be a nice person, with the exception of her stepson Alois Jr. Like Mao, Stalin, and Hussein, Hitler was the only surviving child after previous siblings had died, although during his early years he was often ill. Because of this, Alois often complained to Klara:

"So you have failed me once more! Is it impossible for you to bear me a healthy child?" The words typify the hostile, blaming attitude members of the family saw. (Ibid.)

Alois's pre-conceptual trauma—his illegitimacy, his mother's depression and early death, being fatherless and raised by strangers, and so on—induced such a rage and envy that he felt impelled to attack others in order to humiliate them and make them as unhappy as he had been as a child. Such an unhappy marriage—a husband most of the time absent and who often mistreated her, as well as losing her first three children in a short time—had a determining impact on Klara's temperament; she became dull-looking and withdrawn. Miller (1990) states that Alois, on the other hand, became quarrelsome and irritable.

His main target was Alois Jr. For some time the father … demanded absolute obedience … from his son who refused to give it. Alois Jr. complained bitterly that his father frequently beat him "unmercifully with a hippopotamus whip." Once the boy skipped school for three days to finish building a toy boat. The father, who had encouraged such hobbies, whipped young Alois, then held him against a tree by the back of his neck until he lost consciousness. (Ibid., p. 126)

Paula, Adolf's younger sister, recounts that Adolf also received a similar treatment from his father:

> It was my brother Adolf who specially provoked my father to extreme harshness and who got his due measure of beating every day. He was a rather nasty little fellow, and his father's attempts to beat the impudence out of him and make him choose the career of a civil servant were in vain. (Ibid., p. 127)

Victor (1998) also remarks:

> ... Adolf became very stubborn with his father and, according to his sister Paula, provocative. Probably the repetition of what had happened with his first son was too much for Alois. On discovering this, Alois beat him so badly he went into a coma. For days the family did not know whether he would live. (p. 29)

Many years later Hitler confided to a secretary that once, as a child, he read in an adventure novel that the ability to show no pain was an expression of great courage:

> "I resolved not to make a sound the next time my father whipped me. And when the time came I still can remember my frightened mother standing outside the door. I silently counted the blows. My mother thought I had gone crazy when I beamed proudly and said, "Father hit me thirty-two times!" (Miller, 1990, p. 126)

It might have been a way of Hitler not only trying to calm his mother but also to make her feel that she could trust him as someone who was fearless and capable of confronting his powerful father. Such regular beatings from his father, which possibly started around the age of four, (ibid., p. 160) had serious and deep impacts on Hitler's former character and idiosyncrasy, such as anxiety attacks and recurrent nightmares. Miller states:

> He often wakes up in the middle of the night and wanders restlessly to and fro. Then he must have light everywhere. Lately he has sent at these times for young men who have to keep him company during these hours of manifest anguish. At times his condition

must have been dreadful … Hitler wakes at night with convulsive shrieks. He shouts for help. He sits on the edge of his bed, unable to stir. He shakes with fear, making the whole bed vibrate. He mutters confused, totally unintelligible phrases. He gasps, as if imagining himself to be suffocating. (Ibid., p. 143)

Miller also describes in detail what took place during one of his crises, from the recollection made by someone she described as a "reliable source":

Hitler stood swaying in his room, looking widely about him. "It was he! He's been here!" he gasped. His lips were blue. Sweat streamed down his face. Suddenly he began to reel off figures and odd words and broken phrases, entirely devoid of sense. It sounded horrible … Then he stood quite still, only his lips moving … Then he suddenly burst out: "There, there! In the corner! Who's that?" His stamped and shrieked … He was shown that there was nothing out of the ordinary in the room, and then he gradually grew calm. After that he lay asleep for many hours. (Ibid.)

Adolf Hitler grew up in an environment filled with contradictions, where violence and beatings, justified or not, were part of his every-day life, living in constant threat from his father and, at the same time, experiencing total adoration from his mother who tolerated everything he did; however, she lacked the ability to protect him from his father's cruelty. Hitler lived constrained by three important emotional forces: i) his father's violence; ii) his mother's adoration, and, at the same time, iii) her inability to protect him from his father's violence. These main factors structured Hitler's pre-conceptual trauma, his main idio-syncrasy or Cain's mark (López-Corvo, 2014). These forces were abso-lutely determinant of the way in which he became politically driven in the future.

Father's aggression

The aggression by his father determined the formation of a paranoid structure, as observed in Miller's description, when he woke up at night in a complete terror sensing that an aggressor—perhaps his father— was hiding in his room. Paranoia is a defence used with the purpose of placing the enemy outside, which might have been what his dream was trying to tell him. Choosing the Jews as the "main enemy" was possibly the result of several factors. First, there was the suspicion that his main enemy, his father, was the son of a Jew, meaning that he was not, after all, a pure Aryan. Victor (1998) says:

> He believed Alois was evil and that his evil came from mixed ancestry—from Alois's Jewish father. The prohibition against Jews marrying or engaging in sex with Aryans was meant to prevent someone like his father from being born again. And the obscured prohibition against Jews employing Aryans maids during the childbearing years covered the exact situation in which his father had been conceived, as Hitler understood it. (p. 18)

Hitler also felt that his father had "contaminated" his Aryan mother with his Jewish blood. In the Nuremberg Laws he established thirty limitations of marriage in order to avoid such contamination: Aryan women and girls could not consult Jewish physicians, nor could they shop in Jewish stores, attend the same school, or live in the same building, while Jews could only use "Jewish names" so that they would not deceive "innocent" Aryan girls. According to Victor (ibid., p. 17), Hans Frank, a lawyer from the Nazi party, stated that, in 1930, Hitler called him in and showed him a letter from his nephew, Patrick Hitler, who was trying to blackmail him about his Jewish ancestry.

The father's uncontrollable aggression can also induce splitting in the gender identification of a boy who, out of castration fear, resorts to a feminine identification, or identification with his mother, in order to pacify the angry father.

Mother's adoration

The Treaty of Versailles, signed on 28 June 1919, between Germany and the allied countries (France, Italy, and Britain) established, among other things, that Germany was responsible for starting the First World War and had to pay financial reparation to the allied countries; also, German troops were to be reduced to no more than 100,000 and were prevented from possessing heavy armaments such as tanks, airplanes, warships, and submarines. In order to pay its debt, calculated as 132 billion ($31.5 billion/£6.6 billion), Germany printed an immense amount of money that produced hyperinflation, reducing the German mark to one trillionth of its value. But perhaps what outraged Germany the most was the transference of a large part of its territory to other countries, such as France, Poland, Denmark, Czechoslovakia, and Belgium.

In Hitler's unconscious, Germany very much resembled his beaten, threatened, helpless, and powerless mother that he felt impelled to rescue. Often a mother's dedication towards and adoration of a child is sensed by the child to be an expression of her weakness. Victor described this interaction as follows:

> Reportedly Klara caressed him often and breast-fed him longer than her other children and, when Alois was away, she took Adolf into her bed. Her intimacy with him was obvious ... Klara's attachment to Adolf remained extreme until her death; his attachment to her remained extreme until his death years later. (Ibid., p. 24)

According to Paula, Adolf was very concerned about his mother and when she got ill with breast cancer, he became devoted to her care, overwhelming her with tenderness and extremely attentive to her needs:

> He would watch her every moment so that he might anticipate her slightest need. His eyes, which usually gazed mournfully into the distance, would light up whenever she was relieved of her pain. Apparently he saw himself ... In a desperate struggle to save Klara ... [she] had been the centre of Adolf's life. Her sickness was a grim opportunity to fulfil the role for which his early experiences had prepared him—to save her. Klara held on only a few weeks, dying just before Christmas ... She had been the one in need of rescue, the one to whom it was worth devoting himself. (Ibid., pp. 40–41)

Langer (1972) on the other hand states:

> Germany became a symbol of his ideal mother, and his sentiments are clearly expressed in his writing and speeches. A few excerpts will serve to illustrate the transfer of emotions: "The longing grew stronger to go there (Germany) where since my early youth I had been drawn to secret wishes and secret love ... What I first had looked upon as an impassable chasm now spurred me on to greater love for my country than ever before ... An unnatural separation

> from the great common Motherland ... I appeal to those who, sev-
> ered from the Motherland ... and who now in painful emotions
> long for the hour that will allow them to return to the arms of the
> beloved mother." ... It is significant that although Germans, as a
> whole, invariably refer to Germany as the "Fatherland", Hitler
> almost always refers to it as the "Motherland". (p. 172)

Nazi propaganda targeted the unfairness of the Versailles Treaty, something very much welcomed by the people, but Hitler was the only political leader of his time who continuously not only argued against the
Treaty, but also took action against the conditions it established. He was
even declared "Man of the Year" in 1936 by *Time* magazine.

Mother's incapacity to provide protection from father's aggression

Throughout most of his adult life Hitler displayed strongly ambivalent
feelings towards women. August Kubizek (1976), a close adolescent
friend, described Hitler's platonic relationship with Stephanie Izak,
a young girl he once saw passing by on the street in Linz and immediately fell madly in love with. He developed an almost delusional obses-
sion about spending the rest of his life with her, to the point, according
to Kubizek, that "Stephanie filled his thoughts so completely that everything he said, or did, or planned for the future, was centred around her"
(Kubizek, p. 59).

> Day after day, Adolf returned to the spot where he had caught sight
> of her, and his vigil was rewarded when she sometimes passed. He
> stared at her and occasionally their eyes met; a couple of times she
> smiled at him and once threw him a flower. (Victor, 1998, p. 38)

This was the only, and the closest, contact with her, but this was sufficient on which to build a powerful fantasy, where he conceived all sorts
of dialogues, imagining that she was also in love with him, and sometimes he even thought of kidnapping her. "By romantic telepathy she
already knew his thoughts *and was in agreement with his wishes*" (ibid.,
original emphasis). The idealisation of this girl reached such a level that
Kubizek felt that "any move of hers beyond the rigid limits of conven-
tion would have destroyed the picture of her which Adolf kept in his
heart" (Kubizek, 1976, p. 36), something that happened sometime later

when Stephanie got engaged, which Hitler experienced as a terrible betrayal and, as a result, according to Kubizek, he developed intense hatred against women. Several women are thought to have been Hitler's lovers; among them were Charlotte Lobjoie in 1917, Erna Hanfstaengl in 1920, Maria Reiter in 1925, Geli Raubal also in 1925, and Unity Mitford in 1934. Some of them attempted suicide, such as Eva, Maria, and Unity; others died by suicide, such as his nieces Geli and Unity, also his wife Eva, in a double suicide with Hitler on 30 April 1945, around forty hours after they had been married.

Angela Maria "Geli" Raubal, the daughter of Angela, Hitler's half-sister, was seventeen years old when she met him, when her mother became a housekeeper at the Berghof Villa in 1928. A year later she moved to Hitler's apartment in Munich with the excuse of studying medicine. After rising to power Hitler became extremely possessive and domineering of his niece, and after discovering that she was having an affair with his chauffeur, he fired the chauffeur and increased his control over her even further. After a heated argument, when Hitler refused to let her move to Vienna in order to get married, she killed herself with his pistol while he was away.

Maria Riter, twenty-one years younger than Hitler, became his lover, and attempted suicide by hanging herself after being abandoned by him, although she was saved by her brother-in-law who found her and cut the rope before she died.

Unity Valkyrie Mitford was a young and attractive British aristocrat, who became extremely infatuated with Hitler, and became a strong supporter of Nazism and a hater of Jews. In 1934 she moved to Munich with the excuse of studying German but with the purpose of stalking Hitler. After several months of following him everywhere, she managed to be invited to his table at the Bavaria Tavern; following this she was introduced to Hitler's inner circle and remained close to him for at least five years. After England's declaration of war on Germany on 3 September 1939, Unity went to the English Garden in Munich and shot herself with a gun Hitler had provided her with, but managed to survive. She was hospitalised and visited by Hitler who sent her back to England. She never recovered completely and died nine years later from meningitis, possibly as a result of the presence of the bullet that was never extracted. There are several theories about her suicide attempt; that she made a pact with Hitler to die in order to meet him in the afterlife; that she was desperate because the two countries that she loved most, England and Germany, were going to destroy each other; that because she was madly in love with him, Hitler had insisted on sending her back to her native country.

Eva Brown was seventeen years old when she met Hitler in 1929, but she began seeing him regularly two years later, just after his niece, Angela, had committed suicide. She became part of Hitler's inner circle but did not participate in any public event until 1944 when her sister married an SS officer. In August 1932 she attempted suicide by shooting herself in the chest, although not seriously, with the purpose of getting Hitler's attention. There was a second suicide attempt in May 1935 when she took an overdose of sleeping pills, as a reaction to Hitler's disinterest in her. When someone suggested to Eva that she should hide after the war, she replied: "Do you think I would let him die alone? I would stay with him up until the last moment …" On 30 April 1945, at around 6.30 pm, they both committed suicide at the *Führerbunker*, Hitler by shooting himself with his pistol in the right temple and she by biting into a cyanide capsule.

It is intriguing that all of the women who had a close relationship with Hitler either attempted or committed suicide. They were just adolescents when they met him, attracted by the aura of power that he projected, and acting out their oedipal needs towards the idealised representations of their fathers. This was an unconscious emotional combination that drove them to a phallic adoration similar to the way his mother had conducted herself towards him. At the same time, there were his ambivalent feelings toward the mother who had failed to protect him from his father's extreme aggression, which he later, as an adult, displaced onto his adolescent girlfriends by seducing them and filling them with hope, but later, once he felt in control, cruelly neglecting or completely abandoning them.

CHAPTER TEN

Stalin

Joseph Stalin was born as Iosif Vissarionovich Dzhugashvili, on 21 December 1878 in the city of Gori, province of Tiflis, in Georgia, southern part of the Russian Empire. His parents, Bessarion Jughashvili, also known as Besso, and Ekaterina Gueladze, nicknamed Keke, were illiterate peasants who had migrated from the nearby mountains and settled in Gori, a town in the centre of Georgia where most of the population was poor and the official language was Russian because Georgian was forbidden in schools and seminaries. Bessarion was a cobbler, well-known in the city for his explosive and violent temperament, which earned him the nickname of "Crazy Besso". Service (2004) states:

> Bessarion married nineteen-year old Ekaterina in 1874. Her father had died when she was young and her mother had to get by as best as they could in the little village of Gambareuli. [Keke] … quickly became pregnant. In fact she had two sons before Joseph's arrival. The first was Mikhail, who died when only one year old. Then came Giorgi, but he too died young. Joseph alone survived early childhood. (p. 16)

This terrible situation persuade Keke—although strict and demanding—to be extremely dedicated to the care of Joseph and to be determined that he receive a formal education. His father wanted Joseph to become a shoemaker like himself, but against his wishes Keke registered her son in a religious school. Obviously, if Bessarion had succeeded in his wishes, Russian history would have been quite different.

Keke always made her son feel as if he was someone special, dressing him well and placing great expectations on him, something his father often resented. Service (2004) says:

> It might have been expected that Joseph's mother and father, having suffered the loss of two sons in infancy, would have treated their third with special care and affection. These would also have been in keeping with the Georgian tradition to dote on a new baby in the family. The Georgians are more like the Italians and Greeks than the peoples of northern Europe in child rearing. Bessarion Dzhugashvili was an exception because he never showed his son any kindliness. (Ibid.)

From the very beginning the couple had a difficult relationship, mostly due to Besso's temperament as well as his inclination to alcohol, a condition that was exacerbated by Joseph's birth. Whenever Besso got drunk, which was often, he would become extremely violent, mainly towards his wife but later on also against his son.

His drinking got out of control. He spent more time guzzling wine at Yacob Egnatashvili's tavern than tending to his family obligations … When Stalin was asked, in 1931, about his childhood by the writer Emile Ludwig, he strenuously rebuffed suggestions of mistreatment: "No … My parents were uneducated people but they didn't handle me at all badly." This was out of line with his other recollections. He told his daughter Svetlana about how he stood up to his father and threw a knife at him when Keke was taking yet another beating (Service, ibid., pp. 17–19).

There is no question that, similar to all the totalitarian dictators evaluated in this study, the savage and cruel control later displayed by Stalin against the Russians was a direct consequence of the ambivalent and inconsistent emotional environment in which he grew up, being caught between an overly consenting mother and a physically abusive father. Such inconsistencies represent the core of what we have referred to in the first chapter of this book as the "pre-conceptual trauma".

"No psychoanalytical sophistication is required," says Service. "Like many who have been bullied in childhood, Joseph grew up looking for others whom he could bully" (ibid., p. 19). Stalin witnessed the detention, incarceration, and execution of many of those who were close to him, and becoming his personal friend was a very risky endeavour. He was a megalomaniac, egocentric, paranoid, and a mass murder dictator, as were the other dictators who are evaluated in this study.

Keke, according to several versions, was a very devoted woman, who regularly attended church and consulted religious men; she even had a great desire for Joseph to become a priest and, years later, when Stalin was Russia's dictator, she told a journalist that she would have preferred him to have entered the priesthood. When Joseph was nine, Besso had to move to Tbilisis to work in a factory, an opportunity his mother used to register the boy in the church school in Gori, and, in order to pay for his education, she cleaned houses and washed clothes for wealthier people in the city. Although at that time Besso spent much of his time away from home, whenever he came back he was unpredictably and unfairly brutal with his son. In spite of this, Stalin did well in school, appeared to love reading, and graduated near the top of his class. However, he had a reputation for being provocative towards other classmates and, on some occasions, had discipline problems with the school authorities. Stalin always found refuge in books, mostly in those about heroes, particularly Koba, a character in one of Aleksandr Kazbegi's books with the suggestive name of *Parricide*, who became his champion, to the extent that later Stalin adopted his name, possibly because Koba was a revengeful hero who acted outside of the law.

The environment outside of home did not help either, because in Gori violent gangs of adolescents were very common, and Joseph eventually managed to join them, as he became able to free himself from Keke's control. Apparently, he was always willing to clash with enemy gangs and many of his friends remembered the tricks and dirty ways of fighting he employed in order to win, the strength of his aggressiveness towards his enemies often leading him to disregard the fact that his opponent was larger and stronger than him, often leaving him badly beaten. Physically Stalin was rather misshapen, small in size, his face marked and scarred by smallpox, and he was born with his left arm shorter than his right. As an adult he was five feet four inches tall and during his life his shortness of stature annoyed him to the extent that he always used platform shoes in order to appear taller.

There was a discrepancy between his quarrelsome temperament and his capacity to do well in school, where he was considered a brilliant student. Such incongruity was perhaps the result of his mind being split between a compliant attitude towards his caring mother and a belligerent one towards his aggressive father. This inconsistency—common to most dictators—represented the core of his pre-conceptual trauma and was later reflected in how he handled his country; believing, on the one hand, that, like Koba, his adolescent hero, he was the only saviour of Russia—his "Mother land"—while, on the other, displaying an obsessive and insane appetite for revenge and death. He established the relentless persecution and execution of citizens, relatives, dissidents, faithful old followers, members of the Communist Party who had worked closely with him, and many others, whom he tormented and brutally tortured, mentally as well as physically, to the point of total humiliation and degradation. There were cases of him ordering the execution of a friend, and then carrying his coffin.

Such splitting between a caring aspect and another that was aggressive and resentful was in fact a "narcissistic structure", a concept that is not easy to explain. It did not mean that he was not truly grateful to his mother for what she had done for him, but rather he only cared about that which he decided he ought to care about. In fact, as an adult he was never really concerned about his mother: for over ten years after the Civil War had ended he did not even attempt to contact her, usually asking high ranking Communist Party leaders to look after her instead. He visit her on only one occasion, as he returned from a vacation via Tifflis where his mother lived and who was alerted just one hour before he arrived.

Like Germany to Hitler, Russia became Stalin's "mother in distress" and in need of being rescued (possibly by Koba!), just as he sensed his mother had felt when she was continuously beaten by his aggressive father when he was a child. Pre-revolutionary Russia was truly in distress; there were mostly three kinds of people: peasants, nobles, and czars, where the peasants, abused by the nobles, presented the greatest level of illiteracy and poverty. The first change Lenin introduced was confiscation of private property without compensation, and later, in the early 1920s, he also created the "New Economic Policy". When Stalin took power after Lenin's death, he changed this policy towards total centralisation and control of the economy.

His "caring" for his country as an adult was a type of unconscious symbolical representation of his real mother: yet, and at the same time, it was not; just like the presence of an absence. He was "good" to Russia and the Russians, but narcissistically, always on his terms and according to his needs.

There are accounts of some of Stalin's women. In 1907 he married Ekaterina Svanidze who came from an educated Georgian family and was the sister of a comrade in the revolutionary movement. She died a year later at the age of twenty-two from typhoid fever and, possibly, from total abandonment by her husband, after giving birth to their son Yakov. Brackman (2001) reports that, by 1911, Stalin was living in the house of Maria Kusakova, a widow who was his landlady and who, after finding herself pregnant, accused Stalin of rape. Later she withdrew the charges, probably because he promised to marry her. In the same year of 1911 Stalin returned to Georgia where he met Olga and Sergey Allilyuev, fellow Russian revolutionaries, who sheltered him in their home for a while. According to Montefiore (2003), an intimate relationship was established at that time between Stalin and Olga. He also met their daughter Nadezhda, who he married eight years later when he was forty-one and she eighteen, a circumstance that fed the rumour that his wife was also his daughter. They had two children, Vasily and Svetlana, but with time their marriage turned sour and very conflictual to the extent that on 7 November 1932, during the dinner celebration of the fifteenth anniversary of the revolution at which Stalin nastily flicked cigarettes across the table at her, Nadezhda left the table, went to her bedroom and shot herself through the right temple. Since she was left-handed, there was a rumour that he had killed her, in order to free himself from "a very neurotic and disturbed wife".

There is an account of Stalin having many casual relations with several young women, such as actresses, ballerinas, singers, and so on; however, in 1934 he established a lasting relationship with his housekeeper, Valentina (Valechka) Istomina, a nineteen-year-old peasant girl who became his devoted mistress, considered by many historians as his third wife. She served Stalin from the beginning of 1935 to the time of his death in 1953. Svetlana, Stalin's daughter, described the moment when Valechka came into the room where Stalin's body lay:

> She dropped heavily to her knees, put her head on my father's chest and wailed at the top of her voice as the women in villages do. She went on for a long time and nobody tried to stop her. (Volkogonov, 1990, pp. 553–554)

CHAPTER ELEVEN

Mao

Mao ruled China for twenty-seven years and attempted, in any way he could, to destroy its culture, on the basis that everything could be questioned: country, family, marriage, private property: "Nothing was too outrageous, too shocking or unsayable," say Chang and Halliday (2005, p. 13). They continue:

> ... Mao could never relax his vigilance about his personal safety, and it was from now that he began to perfect the security measures that developed in later life into a truly awesome system. To begin with he had about a hundred guards, and the number grew. He picked several houses in different places ... [that] invariably had escape exits. (pp. 57–57)
> ... Mao had secret dwellings built in secluded valleys ... Few knew of their existence, then or now. Mao's goal, they said, was to become the "Party Emperor". (p. 94)

In the end, Mao was responsible for the deaths of at least seventy million of his fellow citizens.

Mao was born on 26 December of 1893 in a family of peasants from the Valley of Shaoshan, in the province of Hunan, where his ancestors had lived for over 500 years. It is a place known for its beauty, humid climate, and rolling hills where rice, bamboo, and tea are cultivated. His father, Mao Yi-chang (1870–1920) became engaged when he was ten years old and later married a thirteen-year-old girl from a nearby town, who, some said, had no name, as was the custom of the time, and was known as the "Seventh Sister Wen" because that was her order of birth and Wen was the name of her clan (Chang & Halliday, 2005, p. 1); others, however, said her name was Wen Qimei, that she was born in 1867 and died in 1919. They were married in 1885 when she was eighteen years old and Yi-chang was fifteen. Mao was the third child but the first one to survive and his mother, who was devoted to Buddha, became extremely religious in the hope that the gods would protect her surviving child. They named him *Tse-tung*, meaning "the one who shines from the East". Also, as was the habit then, they provided him with a nickname: *Shisan yazi* or the "Child of Stone". Later on, he would truly flaunt the meaning of this moniker:

> Mao's order to cadres was to "confiscate every last single thing" from those picked out as victims. Often whole families were turned out of their homes, and had to go and live in buffalo sheds …

One of Mao's officers, passing by a place, described some of his own relatives he had found there:

> "I went into a big black-tiled bungalow … I was struck by a tremendous air of sadness and desolation … There were two middle-age women and an old woman, plus three young children, all in rags, and looking famished. When they saw me come in with four bodyguards wearing pistols, they went into tremendous panic …"
> (Ibid., p. 107)

The communist saying that "the end justifies the means" was for Mao and some of his followers absolutely paradigmatic. The cruelty, callousness, pitilessness, and total lack of respect for people's lives, mostly the poor, was one of Mao's greatest weapons. In 1948, as a manoeuvre to induce pity and concern in Nationalist forces, in order to lead them either to surrender or to defect, Mao ordered his own army to prevent civilians from abandoning occupied towns. Mao's own words, in relation to one of these cities, was to "turn Changchun into a city of death", the result being that millions died from starvation. Lin Biao, the commander in charge at that time, wrote to Mao about the results of these actions:

> "The starving people knelt in front of our soldiers en masse, begging to be allowed to go. Some put their babies down in front of the troops and turned back themselves, some hanged themselves on the sentry posts. The sentries could not bear the sight of the misery. Some knelt with the starving people and wept with them ... others secretly released refugees. After we corrected this, we discovered another tendency. Soldiers beat up, abused and tied up refugees [to push them back] and went as far as opening fire on refugees, causing deaths." (Ibid., p. 313)

In order to establish control Mao "began systematic terrorisation of the population, to induce long-term conformity and obedience; his methods were uniquely Maoist" (ibid., p. 323). "A young half-Chinese woman from Britain witnessed one rally in the centre of Peking, when some 200 people were paraded and then shot in the head so that their brains splattered out onto bystanders" (ibid., p. 324). It is thought that in labour camps where most of Mao's political opponents were sent, around twenty-seven million died. Persecution of adversaries was based on two categories of enemies: those who attempted rebellion, accused of being bandits; and the others who were considered to be "spies". Another group that Maoists fought were the religious:

> In general religious and quasi-religious organisations were either branded reactionary and suppressed, or brought under tight control. Almost all foreign clergy were expelled, along with most foreign businessmen, virtually clearing China of non-Communist foreigners by about 1953. Non-Communist foreign press and radio were, it goes without saying, banned. (Ibid., p. 327)

On another occasion a veteran in the Red Army described what he and his comrades experienced:

> "[W]hen we entered the city and saw what it was like, we were devastated. Many of us wept. A lot of us said: We're supposed to be fighting for the poor, but these dead here, how many are the rich? Which of them are Nationalists? Aren't they all poor people?" (Ibid., p. 313)

It seemed that the only person to whom Mao ever expressed devotion was his mother. He seemed to love her with a particular feeling he never showed to anybody else; every time he addressed her it was with great emotion and he often stated how proud he was of the nickname she had given him. He remembered how gentle and tolerant she had been with him, that she never raised her voice or punished him. Once, he commented to members of his cabinet that he even became a Buddhist because of her:

> "I worship my mother ... Wherever my mother went, I would follow ... going to temple fairs, burning incense and paper money, doing obeisance to Buddha ... Because my mother believed in Buddha, so did I." (Ibid., p. 5)

We know little about Mao's early childhood. It has been said that during his first eight years he stayed with his mother and her family, several kilometres from the province where his father was living. Apparently, his grandmother, as well as his uncles and their wives, spoiled him so much that he preferred to live with them. At a later age, he remembered this time with pleasure, and referred to those years as idyllic; unfortunately, it ended once he had to move to Shaoshan to live with his father in order to continue his education. This involved a great adjustment to his life, having to give up the pleasant environment of the maternal house in order to spend time with his father, an illiterate peasant, unfriendly, demanding, tough, and strict, who aspired for his son to work the land, as he did.

Confucius's ideas formed part of the local curriculum; however, since this information was rather obscure for children to grasp, they resorted to learning it by heart. Mao, blessed with a prodigious memory, performed this well and his classmates remembered him as someone capable not only of reciting but even writing the difficult texts. He also did well in prose, poetry, and calligraphy, but, at the same time, was rebellious and provocative to the point that he often clashed with teachers and tutors and on three occasions was asked to leave the school. Yi-chang, his father, who paid for his education and laboured all his life, expected from Mao a similar dedication, and resented laziness, indecision, and the choice of a different type of destiny. Mao hated his father, and these feelings were so persistent that in 1968, when planning the great and brutal repression of his political detractors, he remarked to the executors of this revengeful campaign that he would have liked to treat his father with the same brutality: "my father was a bad man. If he were to be alive today, he should be 'jet-planed'" (ibid., p. 6).[1] Little is known about what could have induced such hatred of a father by a son; there is no doubt, however, that those revengeful feelings absolutely structured Mao's character and attitude towards others, a condition we can find in almost all totalitarian dictators.

Later, Mao became more sensitive and paranoid towards any form of criticism, usually reacting, as any other totalitarian dictator, with great cruelty and aggression towards anyone who dared to criticise him. There is, for instance, the case of Wang Shiwei, a communist journalist who wrote mainly for the revolutionary youth, and who said of them that their dreams were shattered because of "institutionalised privilege, accompanied by high-handedness and arrogance". He wrote:

> I am not egalitarian. But I do not think it is necessary or justified to have multiple grades of food or clothing ... If, while the sick can't even have a sip of noodle soup ... some quite healthy big shots are indulging in extremely unnecessary and unjustified perks, the lower ranks will be alienated. (Ibid., p. 242)

When Mao read Shiwei's comments, he reacted with great anger:

> ... he slammed the newspaper on his desk and demanded angrily: "Who is in charge here? Wang Shiwei, or Marxism?" He picked up the phone and ordered a shape-up at *Liberation Daily*. (Ibid.)

Mao complained:

> "Many people rushed from far away to ... read his article [publicly posted]. But no one wants to read mine!" (Ibid., p. 243)

Some conversational remarks to friends about Shiwei preferring Trotsky to Stalin, were enough to send him to prison.

> In 1944, when some journalists ... were allowed ... he was wheeled out to meet them and produced a robotic confession, as if he had been brain washed: "He said over and over again: 'I'm a Trotskyite.

> I attacked Mao. I deserve to be executed … But Mao is so magnani-
> mous … I am extremely grateful for his mercy.'" When the Commu-
> nists evacuated Yenan in 1947, he [Shiwei] was taken along—and
> executed en route. One night he was hacked to death and thrown
> into a dry well. He was forty-one. (Ibid.)

In 1933 Mao was very ill with malaria and asked for Dr Nelson Fu,
who had looked after him ten years earlier. "Patient and doctor both
knew Fu had saved Mao's life—and his political fortunes" at that time.
(p. 127). Dr Fu remained his doctor for many years. However, in 1966,
during Mao's "Great Purge", he wrote to Mao reminding him of the
time he had treated him for malaria: "I saved your life, I hope you save
mine now."

> The then seventy-two-year-old had been savagely beaten, his ribs
> broken, and his skull fractured. Mao did lift a finger, but not very
> forcefully, by minuting on Fu's letter: "This man … has not com-
> mitted big crimes, perhaps he should be spared." But then he heard
> that Fu had allegedly talked to other Party leaders about his [Mao's]
> health, which was a big taboo for Mao. Mao let Fu be thrown into
> prison. The septuagenarian doctor did not last two weeks, and died
> on the floor of his cell. (Ibid., p. 127)

Similar fates were suffered by Mao's brother Tse-min, who had been
killed at the beginning of 1940, "partly as the result of Mao's giving
instructions not to try to save him when he was in prison" (p. 609), and
by his second wife who was executed after being abandoned by Mao.

Although information about the relationship between Mao and his
father is rather scarce, we know that, in contrast to his mother and his
maternal relatives, Yi-chang used to beat, belittle, and insult his son frequently. Once, Mao confronted his father and was able to tell him that,
being older, he should be capable of performing heavy physical work
rather than him, who was much younger; this was an attitude considered disrespectful by the standards of Chinese culture at that time. One
day, according to Mao, he had a bitter argument with his father in front
of some guests:

> "My father scolded me before them, calling me lazy and useless.
> This infuriated me. I called him names and left the house … My

father … pursued me, cursing as well as commanding me to come back. I reached the edge of a pond and threatened to jump in if he came any nearer … My father backed down." … Retelling the story, he laughed and added …: "Old men like him didn't want to lose their sons. This is their weakness. I attacked at his weak point, and I won!" (Ibid., p. 6).

Mao appeared to be very ambivalent about women; there is a great discrepancy between the feelings he claimed to experience about his mother and those that he openly and continuously exercised against his own wives. Remembering his mother's death that took place in 1919, he declared:

"When my mother was dying, I told her I could not bear to see her looking in agony. I wanted to keep a beautiful image of her, and told her I wanted to stay away for a while. My mother was a very understanding person, and she agreed. So the image of my mother in my mind has always been and still is today a healthy and beautiful one." (Ibid., p. 18)

This attitude towards his mother's death very much contrasted with the manner in which he responded to his father passing away:

Less surprisingly, Mao treated his dying father coldly. Yi-chang died from typhoid on 23 January 1920, and before his death he longed to see his oldest son, but Mao stayed away, and showed no feelings of sadness for him. (Ibid.)

Mao, however, did not learn from his own experience and was as callous and cruel to his wives and children as his father had been with him. He married four times, although he never parented his children, who very often died in infancy or were sent away. He always left his wives behind as he travelled through China, ignoring them to the extent that he allowed one of his followers to shoot one of them, without making any moves to prevent it. The Nationalist enemies of Mao later executed Yang Kahui, Mao's second wife, who had been deserted by him along with their two children. Kahui left behind distressing documents describing her disillusionment with communism and with her husband, whom she loved. Gui-yuan, Mao's third wife, became very disheartened by his compulsive unbearable womanising. According to her:

> Over their marriage of nearly ten years, she had had to live with her husband's heartlessness. She was particularly hurt by his callousness towards her painful pregnancies and childbirth ... and by his crack that she gave birth to babies "as easily as a hen dropping eggs". And she was bitter that although he was indifferent to children, and had not cared when four of theirs had died or been abandoned, he repeatedly made her pregnant ... She felt no affection from Mao and when their baby was born, she wrote to him saying that the child resembled him closely, but received no reply, not then nor after the child had died ... Two years after ... Gui-yuan learned by chance that Mao had remarried. (Ibid., pp. 195–196)

When Mao turned fourteen, his father refused to continue paying for his studies and forced him to do labouring work, something that he hated. However, this did not last long, because Mao found his way out by consenting, if his father continued paying for his studies, to marry a cousin who was four years his senior. Her family name was Lou, but since she did not have a first name, she was addressed as "woman Lou". Mao's father believed that this marriage was going to make his son settle down and help him to give up his crazy ideas of going to school, so that he would finally dedicate himself to labouring work. However, destiny had different plans and Lou died shortly afterwards, allowing Mao to be free again and, also, creating in him a hatred of arranged marriage for the rest of his life:

> Nine years later, he wrote a seething article against the practice: "In families in the West, parents acknowledge the free will of their children. But in China, orders from the parents are not at all compatible with the will of the children ... This is a kind of 'indirect rape.' Chinese parents are all the time indirectly raping their children ..." (Ibid., p. 7)

Because his father once again refused to continue paying for his studies, Mao turned to his mother and maternal relatives for help, and

they managed to convince Yi-chang to prolong his financial support—
something he did for a short time although long enough to allow Mao
to find a way out and to register in a new school especially created
for young people. It was a time of social transformation in the history
of China, which included the creation of a new educational system.
Paradoxically, the opportunities that were open to Mao in 1911 were
completely different from those produced during Mao's totalitarian
communist regime, when teaching was mostly reduced to primary
schools known as "Lenin schools", where children were taught only
to read and write. The majority of secondary schools were abolished
and their buildings used for political purposes. Children were trained
to become "Red Guards" in order to attack the "Four Olds" of Society:
"old customs, old culture, old habits, and old ideas." They marched
across China in order to abolish these "Four Olds"; so old books and
old art were destroyed, museums, famous temples, and shrines where
ransacked, and streets renamed with revolutionary names as well as
adorned with pictures of Mao. A great number of historical monuments,
the most outstanding manifestation of the nation's civilisation, which
had so far survived Mao's loathing, were demolished. In Peking, of the
6,843 monuments that were standing in 1958, 4,922 were completely
obliterated (ibid., p. 521).

> All adults except the very old and crippled were put into the Red
> Defence Army. In this way, the entire population was regimented,
> and a web of control was formed. (Ibid., p. 104)

These kinds of "clash troops" were also trained to harass people in order
to make them join the Army, or, for those who had deserted, to return
them to the army's ranks.

> On 24 August [1966], national police chief Xie Fuzhi told his sub-
> ordinates to pass out information clearly responding to questions
> like: "What if the Red Guards kill these people?" Xie said: "If people
> are beaten to death … it is none of our business … Don't be bound
> by rules set in the past … if you detain those who beat people to
> death … you will be making a big mistake." Xie assured his reluc-
> tant subordinates: "Premier Chou [Vice-president] supports it".
> (Ibid., p. 519)

In other words, the same cruelty, bigotry, and reluctance his father expressed towards Mao's ambitions and academic education, was afterwards implemented by him on millions of Chinese children who, from early in life, were taught only military strategies about how to fight and annihilate the enemy.

The amount of callousness and sadism exercised by Mao and his wife against people who served them and were close to them was notorious. When Mao's premier, Chou En-lai, was diagnosed with cancer of the bladder, the doctors recommended immediate surgery due to the incipiency of the illness. However, they were forced to report first to Mao, who then, being in need of Chou to deal with some foreign affairs, told them: "First: keep it secret, and don't tell the premier or [his wife]. Second: no examination. Third: no surgery ..." (ibid., p. 592). Several months later Chou's condition had deteriorated: his urine contained a lot of blood, a sign that the tumour had critically worsened. But when the doctors pleaded to be allowed to conduct a full examination and give him treatment, Mao rebuked them through his chamberlain on 7 February, using words to the effect that Chou was quite old enough to die; adding: "What the hell do you want an examination for?" (ibid., p. 594).

Many of those people who were captured were also tortured to death in their own homes. Some were taken to improvised "torture chambers", such as old cinema theatres and sports stadiums. Mao eventually succeeded in wiping out the culture and traditions of the Chinese people. He did what he could to achieve his long-held goal of expunging China's past from the minds of his subjects.

Like many other dictators, such as Castro, Mao exhibited a proclivity for manipulation of the press, for instance, generating a rumour about his own death or attempting to place the "internal persecutor" outside:

> On 15 April 1932, the Communists issued a declaration of war on Japan. This was a pure propaganda stunt, and it was more than five years before the Red Army fired a shot at the Japanese ... making this one of the longest "phony wars" in history. (Ibid., p. 113n)

Japan became something similar to what the USA represented to Castro, an enemy created s outside in order to make people unite around their leader:

> As with Long March, the Reds pretended that the goal was to fight the Japanese, and called it the "Anti-Japanese Vanguard", with

slogans like "Going easy to fight Japan". But this was pure propaganda. Mao's Force did not even try to get near the Japanese.
(Ibid., p. 173n)

Castro—who never visited China during Mao's life—and Che Guevara,
did not get along with Mao, because they refused to side with him
against Russia. Castro referred to Mao as "a shit" and accused Peking
"in front of a large international audience ... of applying economic pressure to try to lever him away from Moscow" (ibid., p. 572).

Similar to other totalitarian regimes, Mao lavishly disposed of
millions of dollars for the purpose of exercising grandiosity, while
his people were often on the verge of starvation; in 1960 alone over
twenty-two million people died of starvation in China. When Che
Guevara went to China in November 1960, Mao gave him US $60 million
as a "loan", which Chou told Guevara he "did not have to be repay"
(ibid., p. 461):

> ... While Mao dished out money and food, and built expensive
> underground railway systems, shipyards and infrastructure for
> countries far richer than China, most of the 900 million Chinese
> hovered just above survival levels ... In the years 1971–75, foreign
> aid took up a staggering average of 5.88 per cent of China's entire
> expenditure, peaking at 6.92 per cent in 1973—by far the highest
> percentage in the world, and at least seventy times the U.S. level ...
> Mao made sure that for the vast majority of its population, China
> remain a tightly sealed prison." (Ibid., p. 586)

Mao also spent a great amount of money trying to split the Communist
Party by creating Maoist parties around the world:

> ... Albanian archives reveal a tetchy Kang [Mao's intelligence
> chief] in Tirana griping about Venezuelan leftist walking off with
> U.S. $ 300.000 of China's money funnelled through Albania.
> (Ibid., p. 462)
>
> Thanks to food donated by China, the Albanians did not even
> know what rationing was, while the Chinese were dying in their
> tens of millions. Albania's chief negotiator with Peking, Pupo Shyti,
> said that, at that time, "in China you could see the famine ... But
> the Chinese gave us everything ... When we needed anything, we
> asked the Chinese ... I felt ashamed ... " (Ibid., p. 461)

Besides Albania, Mao provided help to Hungary, Algeria, Cuba, Venezuela, and Thailand. Mao's ultimate ambition was to dominate the world. In 1968, he said:

> "In my opinion, the world needs to be unified ... In the past, many including the Mongols, the Romans ... Alexander the Great, Napoleon, and the British Empire, wanted to unify the world. Today, both the Unites States and the Soviet Union want to unify the world. Hitler wanted to unify the world ... But they all failed. It seems to me that the possibility of unifying the world has not disappeared ... In my view, the world can be unified." (Ibid., p. 565)

CHAPTER TWELVE

Castro

Fidel Castro was born on 13 August 1926 in the province of Banes, in Biran, a small town that could only be reached by horse. He was the illegitimate child of Angel Castro, an illiterate Gallego of humble extraction originally from Lugo, in Spain, who, attempting to escape from the misery of his family, joined the army as a young man and was sent to Cuba to defend the Spanish Crown from *"independentists"* who had taken cover in the Eastern Sierra of the island. Once the control of the Spanish Crown was over, Angel Castro established himself in Cuba as a worker for the United Fruit Company.

He managed to buy land and at other times to steal from neighbours to the point where he had amassed in a short time a significant amount of wealth and also a reputation for being ruthless as well as a thief, who was willing to resolve differences with guns rather than by legal means. Following the advice of Fidel Pino, a fellow countryman who told him that a businessman like him could not also be illiterate, he hired Maria Luisa Argota, a governess from the region's North American school. She was a pleasant and friendly person who eventually married him and gave birth to two children. After two years of marriage, Angel impregnated a young mixed-race girl who worked in his house as a maid and who was the same age as his daughter Lidia; her name was Lina Ruz.

When Maria Luisa found out, she asked for a divorce, but Angel, not wanting to split his property, declared himself bankrupt, and, in order to cover things up, sent Lina away to live with her parents; by the time she left she had already had three children with Angel. After a while, and again on the advice of Angel's friend Pino, the children were taken away from their mother and sent to Havana; Fidel, who was then four years old, was placed with the Hipolytes, a black family from Haiti known for their tendency to use physical punishment to discipline children. Four years later, at the age of eight, it was decided that Fidel should enter a Catholic boarding school, but he was rejected on account of not being baptised, a sacrament denied at that time to children who were born out of wedlock. Fidel Pino interceded with the religious authorities and Fidel Castro was finally accepted. He could visit his mother only at Christmas, but was never allowed to visit "Las Manacas", his father's large house; he saw his father on only a few occasions and from a distance, when Angel was inspecting his land on horseback.

At the age of eight Fidel was finally baptised; however, since his father had not yet legally recognised him as his son, he was registered as Fidel Hipolyte Ruz, taking the name of the Haitian family he had previously stayed with. Sometime later, his siblings joined him at the boarding school—Ramon the older and Raul, who, being the youngest was protected by Fidel, mostly because, being rather timid, he was often teased by his schoolmates. Years later Raul surrendered his country to the Red Army when he signed a secret agreement in Moscow to allow the USSR to deploy missiles with nuclear warheads on the island.

It would not have been easy to have been born in Cuba at the beginning of the twentieth century, in a country that was essentially Catholic, if you were an illegitimate child not having been baptised, as was demanded by the church, being at the same time fatherless and a boarder at a very early age in a Catholic school located at a great distance from your mother's home. Obviously, Fidel felt himself completely abandoned, unwanted, rejected by everybody, his mother, his father, the church, the priests, and even the Haitian family who he spent some time with and whose name he was still using, although he intensely despised it. It might have been difficult to live in a religious boarding school for high and middle class white children, when you were illegitimate, poor, fatherless, not baptised, and using the name of a black family. In time Fidel became rather paranoid and very aggressive, extremely envious of those classmates who were able to have everything they wanted, while he had so little. The three brothers, who often ganged up on other children, were feared and considered the school's hooligans. In 1935, the school authorities decided not to take them back the following school year and Lina, their mother, had to come from Biran to collect them. Fidel never forgot the date of 7 January 1936, as it was the first time he visited his father's house; however, when it was decided that he should remain and be educated there, he strongly objected. He was taken to Santiago again, although this time he was placed in a Jesuit school and felt comfortable for the first time: "he considered that he had finally found his family" (Raffy, 2004, p. 40).

By the age of fifteen he was finally legally recognised by his father and was able to change his name from Hypolite, which he hated, to Castro, a change that allowed him to enter the Jesuit college of Belen in Havana, the place where the social elite of Cuba were educated. From very early on, Fidel showed a strong determination to win, to always be first at school, in the first row; it was a sickly ambition for success, and he was unable to contain frustration, where any form of failure drove him completely mad and capable of doing anything in order to win. He was named "el Loco" meaning "the crazy one", and at other times "el Bicho" or "the bug", although it also meant depraved and wicked, possibly due to his paranoid behaviour of being chronically tormented and in a continuous state of excitement as well as extreme aggression. There is no question that at this early age Fidel was acting out his own pre-conceptual trauma, the early abandonment and rejection from both parents, a sense of helplessness and tremendous envy towards his well-to-do classmates. Fidel never felt loved by his father and when his father died at the age of eighty-one, it had been a long time since they had seen or spoken to each other. Fidel's memories of him were of an extremely angry individual, always touring his hacienda on a white horse, unmoved, pompous, and very engaged in the administration of his land. Not even once did he express any tenderness towards his children. Like Hitler, Stalin, and Mao, Castro felt rejected by his ruthless father and abandoned by his weak mother; they became phantasies and emotions that he later displaced: the powerful rejecting father into the US, or the Empire, as he often referred to it, and his debased and helpless mother into Cuba, his motherland, which he felt needed "liberation" and to be possessed; something he did for over fifty years.

In 1945 Fidel entered the school of law at the University of Havana, where he became a political activist, president of the students' federation and part of the violent culture of "gangsterism", meaning that when he was unable to dominate a situation with words he would resort to weapons, just as his father did. According to Raffy (ibid., p. 320), Fidel gained the reputation of being like a gangster, a liar, someone who could not be trusted and well-known for his violence, individualism, and intense thirst for glory.

After overthrowing Baptista and acquiring complete control over his country, he had also to deal with the continuous struggle in his mind between an intelligent and sensitive understanding, as an expression of his non-traumatised state, while in the traumatised there was a continuous pressure to act out his unresolved early and inner need for revenge. Initially he meant well, influenced by logic, common sense, and his desire for social justice against the abuse exercised by the rich against the lower classes. However, as time went by, under the flag of Marxism and communism, the extremely envious and revengeful "Fidel Hypolite", together with the rest of his family and comrades, devoted himself to systematically destroying the economy of his country to the point of total devastation.

We have learned from history that the main difficulty in any attempt to establish a socialist system, based on the fair distribution of wealth, is the discrepancy between the beauty of the theory as it was established by Marx in his *Manifesto* and the fact that those individuals who attempt to put it into practice are always primarily motivated by their inner narcissistic resentment, envy, and a powerful thirst for absolute power and "revengeful hope".

CHAPTER THIRTEEN

Hussein

The territory known today as Iraq was in the past just a fraction of the geographic conglomerate then known as the Ottoman Empire. During the First World War, the United Kingdom declared hostilities against the Turks and their armada in Iraq, ending one hundred years of domination and creating the state of Iraq. However, the British established a monarchy by appointing Faisal II from the Hashemite family as the King of Iraq with the agreement that the country's natural resources, such as oil, could be used for the benefit of the West.

It was around this time, in 1937, that Saddam Hussein was born, in the small town of Al Awaja, located on the west bank of the Tigris River, eight miles south of Tigrit and north of Baghdad. It was a wasteland inhabited by a handful of Bedouins, with mud houses, no electricity or running water, dusty streets, and opportunities only for misery and robbery. Subha Tulfah al-Mussallat (1910–1982), a Bedouin, woman from Tigrit, was Saddam Hussein's mother; of his father, Hussein Abid al-Majid, little is known, since he died a few months after his son was born. Shortly after his death, Subha remarried a cousin, Ibrahim Hassan, an illiterate burglar who was known in the community as "the Liar", who never worked and spent most of his time in coffee shops. Pictures taken at that time showed him holding a rifle and wearing a dagger.

99

Many years later, after Saddam became the most powerful man in Iraq, there was a popular picture of him holding a rifle.

The early years of Saddam's life were not easy. His older brother died of cancer at the age of thirteen, and Saddam was sent as an infant to stay with his uncle Khairallah Talfah—a passionate politician and Nationalist—until he was three years old, because his stepfather considered him a hindrance. It could have been quite traumatic for an infant to experience so many emotional upheavals in such a short period of time: the death of his father, the presence of his stepfather as well as three step-brothers, being separated from his mother who was unable to protect him, and having to stay in a new environment with an unknown man. It is possible that Saddam's later inclination towards politics resulted from an identification with this uncle, an officer from Iraq's Royal Army, who supported the idea of a free and unified Arab country strong enough to defy Western powers and who hated the monarchy, which he considered to be pro-Western.

At the age of five, Saddam returned to his maternal household in Al Awaja because his uncle, Khairallah, was imprisoned by the government; it was a change that structured the character of the future despot. His stepfather, "the Liar", spent his time insulting, humiliating, and punishing Saddam on a daily basis. Early each morning he would kick him awake so that Saddam could help him steal chickens and goats from neighbours. Any "wrongdoing" was severely punished by a beating with a stick smeared in asphalt to make it more effective. It was a ritual performed in the middle of the street; the boy, in order to avoid the whipping, would jump and scream continuously, as if performing some kind of a macabre dance. Many years later when he was Iraq's strong man, Saddam exercised a similarly humiliating practice by forcing people to jump over the bodies of their relatives who lay inert on the floor after having been killed by the regime. After his uncle was released from jail, Saddam asked to live with him again, something that was denied him by his stepfather, because now, different from the time he was a little boy, he was very useful to "the Liar's" rogueries. Sometime later, when Saddam was around ten years of age, he escaped in order to live with his uncle in Tigrit, six miles from his home; to travel such a distance in spite of all the dangers he might have to face required a great amount of daring for a boy his age; he was already living up to the name his mother had given him, *Saddam*, which in Arabic means "the one who confronts".

In 1950 Saddam moved with his uncle and cousins to the slums of Baghdad, a decision that exposed him to greater political activity. Influenced by his uncle, a fanatic Sunni and a veteran of the 1941 Anglo-Iraqi war, Saddam decided to join the army; however, due to his poor academic background he was rejected, which he experienced as shameful, mostly because many relatives from his father's side had been members of the army in the past as well as the present. After he had raced to power, he continuously provided himself with all sorts of military honours, ranks, and awards, perhaps as a form of compensation or revenge for his earlier humiliation. It is believed that this megalomaniacal attitude was responsible for the death of many Iraqi soldiers, because, although he declared himself a "Field Marshal", while at war he would not listen to any strategic advice from any of his true generals.

After he finished high school he attended the school of law, but only for three years, because he abandoned it at the age of twenty to work as a high school teacher and to join the pan-Arab Ba'ath, his uncle's political party. In 1958, a year after he joined the Ba'ath, General Qasim led a coup that overthrew Iraqi King Faisal II. Qasim then associated with the Communist Party, which was completely against the idea of the pan-Arab movement; this decision embittered the militants of the Ba'ath party, who decided to assassinate Qasim. A group of activists, including Saddam, was chosen to ambush and kill Qasim; however, unexpectedly his driver was killed and Qasim was wounded but survived his injuries. Some of the conspirators were jailed, although Saddam managed to escape to Syria and then to Egypt where he remained until 1963. After returning in 1964, Saddam was imprisoned until he managed to escape in 1967. A year later he participated in a bloodless coup that overthrew Iraq's president and appointed a new president, with Saddam as his deputy. In 1976 he became a general in the Iraqi army and rapidly became the strongman of the government.

CHAPTER FOURTEEN

Beethoven

You can no longer be a man, nor for you or for the others.
—Beethoven (first line of his *Tagebuch* (diary))

In the eighteenth century Germany was a fragmented confederation of small feudal territories controlled by their respective sovereigns, which were centred on three main cities: Berlin, Vienna, and Bonn. The court of Cologne was in Bonn and owed fidelity to the Hapsburgs in Vienna. Ludwig van Beethoven (1770–1827) was born in Cologne to a family of musicians; his paternal grandfather, Ludwig also, was an immigrant from Flanders who established himself there, on the other side of the Rhine, moved by the good music, the fine dance, and the sophistication of the court. He became part of the church's school choir where he played the piano and later became its director, until the end of his life. Beethoven's father, Johann, also a musician, a tenor and a music teacher, who learned to sing from his own father, as well as to play the harpsichord and the violin, was part of the church choir too. It was no surprise that Beethoven also entered the field of music; in fact, it had been the custom for hundreds of years for children to enter the professions of their parents.

Beethoven's parents, Johann (1740–1792) and Mary Magdalene van Beethoven (1746–1787), had seven children, of which only three boys survived; Ludwig was the eldest. Maria went through a significant depression after the death of her first child at only six days. There were two important facts that marked Beethoven's life: one was the year of his birth and the other was with regard to his paternity. Although he always claimed to have been born in December 1772, his baptismal certificate indicated that he was born on 17 December 1770. Beethoven declared several times that it was a mistake, because he had been confused with his older, deceased brother, who had the same name. The second confusion was about his lineage, because there was a belief, asserted by many, that he was the illegitimate son of Frederick II, "the Great", King of Prussia; this information was originally published in 1810 and later produced in encyclopaedias, dictionaries, and even music journals. Several friends and relatives exhorted Beethoven to publicly deny such allegations, but the composer never acted against or authorised anybody to refute them. What could have induced him to deny his own father and to dishonour his mother? Was his total dedication to music the reason for his complete indifference about dealing with such accusations? Or did he harbour a secret fantasy of being a blood relative to the greatest noble lineage of his time, to replace the grey and mediocre stature of his drunken father for a loftier figure? After all, maternity is a concrete and corroborated fact, as distinct from paternity, which in the past required an act of faith, and today the aid of scientific testimony. *Pater semper incertus est*, or in the words of Telemachus to Athena, which were underlined by Beethoven in his *Odyssey* (Book I, p. 214):

> My mother said that he is my father;
> but I do not know it,
> because a man never knows who begot him.

It might also be possible that this fancy "family romance" was a consequence of his parents' attitude, that his mother, being unsatisfied with her marriage, shared with her young son her desire to have been married to someone better, often belittling the child's father, and inducing in Beethoven ambivalent feelings towards him. Beethoven's father, on the other hand, aware of the success Mozart had as a young child, may have wished his son to be successful too. Beethoven's father cruelly made young Ludwig practice for hours at a time and imagined that he could make the family rich, to become their "rescuer". After long nights of drinking, Beethoven's father would sometimes drag his son out of bed to practice the piano or play for guests. Young Ludwig gave his first public performance when he was just seven years old.

From very early on, conflicts and tragedy marked Beethoven's family life; his father Johann, who was an only child, became an alcoholic, possibly identifying with his own alcoholic mother, who ended her days committed to a convent in Cologne when Johann was only twelve years old. According to Gottfried Fisher, Beethoven's neighbour, after his grandmother had been taken to the convent his grandfather, Ludwig, became very aggressive, intolerant, critical, and despotic towards Johann, usually making fun of and belittling him. The only form of rebellion Johann ever expressed to his father was to marry Maria Magdalena Keverich, Bethoven's mother, since, at the age of eighteen, and already a widowed mother and working as a maid for a wealthy family, she was considered unfit. After Ludwig's death, Johann's inclination to drink increased to the point that he spent most of his time in taverns and in time was considered a person of questionable reputation. In January 1793, shortly after Johann's death, the Elector ironically wrote to von Shall, a Marshal from the Court, that "the liquor's income tax had suffered a great loss!" This picture of mediocrity and limitation relating to Johann contrasted with the idealisation the family felt towards the old Ludwig, the paternal grandfather, which reached the level of a cult, also elevated by Beethoven's mother, who remembered the pecuniary abundance at the time when her father-in-law worked as *Kapellmeister* to the Court. It is possible that Beethoven, with the help of his mother, resorted to identifying with his grandfather's industriousness instead of with his aggressive and diminished father.

At the age of fourteen Beethoven petitioned the court to be formally appointed as an assistant to the church choir, due to his father's incapacity to support the family. Johann treated his own son in a similar way to how he had been treated as a child by his father; he was a violent father who became Beethoven's teacher, demanding absolute perfection from his playing and often accusing him of being a total embarrassment to the family. According to Solomon (1977),[1] a family friend who witnessed Johann teaching music to his son, stated that

> "Beethoven's father often made use of violence and there were only few days that he wasn't punished in order to force him to play the

piano ... the father was not only rigorous but cruel ... treated him ruthlessly ... and sometimes locked him in the basement ... Other times, when coming home late from the tavern, he would harshly wake up his son, who was unable to understand what was going on, and force him to play until the morning, while he cried." (p. 37)

Solomon also made the important statement that Johann's main interest in his son's performance was based on his own narcissistic needs to be recognised as the father of a child prodigy; however, at the same time, being himself a rather mediocre musician, he feared that Beethoven would surpass his abilities. He invited musicians from Bonn and the court to hear his son's musical performance in his own house and, sometimes, even charged for the attendance. Being in charge of teaching the child it is quite possible he was trying to limit his learning, and this might explain why Beethoven's main expression of creativity, of spontaneous improvisation, was promptly prohibited by his father. Solomon states that:

> ... at a given moment, when he was playing a musical score, his father came in and said: "What is this trash you are playing now? You know that I cannot stand that; play according to the notes, otherwise, your manipulation will not serve you too much." (Ibid., p. 38)

And at other times, when he had visitors and was again improvising by playing the piano with his right hand, his father said to him, "Again this little game? Get out or I will pull your ears off" (ibid.).

It would have been natural for a child, being confused and desperate in the face of such an irregular relationship with his father, to have turned toward his mother in search of love and solace. However, there is no evidence that Beethoven's mother ever protested against the Johann's mistreatment of his son; on the contrary, according to Solomon, there are records that indicate that Maria Magdalena did not show her son enough attention, which might have compensated for the negative consequences of his father's abuse. Cacilia Fisher, according to Solomon, once observed that Beethoven's children "always looked unkempt and most of the time were left in the hands of nannies". It is quite possible that Beethoven's latter difficulties with women—not being able to

cultivate a lasting relationship and even dying single—were a consequence of an early unsatisfied relationship with his mother.

Solomon (ibid.) refers to a harsh note from Würzer, the Elector's
adviser, who after visiting Beethoven's school during the decade of the
1770s, wrote the following about his looks: "It seems that his mother
had already died, because Ludwig v. B. characterised himself by filth
and negligence ..." (pp. 40–41) These remarks suggest that perhaps
Beethoven was neglected by both parents. In spite of Johann's insen-
sitivity towards the teaching of his son, there are records that portray
concern and tenderness by Beethoven towards his father, and Solomon
(ibid.) expressed these matters as follows:

> Led by Beethoven, the three children used to search for their
> drunken father and convince him to quietly return to their house
> with them; and Stephen von Beethoven saw Ludwig "desperately
> interceding with the police to avoid his father being incarcerated".
> Ries said that Beethoven "rarely talked against his father and if he
> did it, he did it unwillingly"; but if "a third party ever expressed a
> hard word against Johann, Beethoven would react angrily." (p. 39)

In some ways Beethoven's early life resembles those of some of the totalitarian leaders, possibly as a consequence of the time in which he lived,
such as the death of previous siblings, the father being a drunkard or the
violence he displayed toward his son; nevertheless, there are important
differences between Beethoven and those in the other group. Johann's
aggressive attitude toward his son was more about the father's concern that his son receive a proper musical training, lacking the brutality
and cruelty often observed in the experiences of the group of dictators.
In addition, his mother was a woman of certain experience; by the time
she married Johann she was already a widow and had given birth to a
boy, unlike the young and inexperienced mothers from the other group.
Neither are there records of Johann being abusive towards Maria, as has
been often observed in the group of autocrats, a condition that usually
induces in children, very often the older boy, the need to rescue the mother
from the father's abuse, and, later on, if they become the ruler of a country, the unconscious need to bring that country to the verge of collapse in
order to endlessly repeat the condition they experienced as a child, when
they wished so powerfully to become their mothers' rescuers.

Although Maria Magdalena often complained about Johann's expenditures due to his drinking as well as about being left at home alone while he went to the tavern, there was also, at the same time,—a certain complicity with her husband's addiction, something common in partners or co-dependents of alcoholics:

> When he received his monthly salary or money paid by his students and came back to his house, he would play a joke; he would throw the money at his wife's feet and say: "Now woman manage yourself with that." Then she gave him a bottle of wine and said: "We couldn't allow men to come home with empty hands." And he added: "Yes, with empty hands!" And she answered: "Yes, but I know you prefer a full glass than an empty one!" "Yes, yes the woman is right, she is always right." (Ibid., p. 33)

It was said that Maria Magdalena was a "sagacious woman who talked and replied with effectiveness, courtesy and moderation to the noble as to the lowly, and because of that she enjoyed great sympathy and respect" (ibid.). She was not considered shy; on the contrary, she often conveyed an alive and argumentative discourse.

At a later age, when Beethoven was an adult, most of his friends agreed that he remembered his mother with "a filial and fervent gratitude", always referred to her "with love and sentiment, and often said that she was an honest and good hearted women". In a letter written to a friend shortly after his mother's death in 1787, Beethoven said: "She was for me a good and caring mother, even my best friend. Who could have been happier than me when I was yet capable of pronouncing the sweet name of my mother and she could hear and answer? Who shall I address now? To the clumsy imitations of her person, product of my imagination? (ibid., p. 39).

When he arrived in Vienna, Beethoven was in his early twenties, and in a short time became a well-known pianist and teacher, tutoring young women from the Austrian nobility. There are records that Beethoven became infatuated with several of these women and even wrote love letters and dedicated sonatas to them; however, he was never capable of establishing a lasting loving relationship with any of them. In 1794 he wrote to Nikolaus Simrock in Bonn asking for his help in finding a wife: "If your daughters are already adults, give me one for a wife. Because, if I were to live in Bonn as a single man, I will not remain there for too long.

No doubt, you will be now feeling the anxiety" (ibid., p. 114). This last remark, about his friend "feeling the anxiety" of being single, but not him, reminds us of the attitude often displayed by adolescents, who feel that their lives and concerns belong to their parents and not to themselves.

Fifteen years later, he made a similar request to another friend who lived in Freiburg: "Now you could help me to find a wife. Even more, you could find a beautiful young one in Freiburg" (ibid., p. 113). From these requests, it seems that Beethoven did not have a great deal of confidence in his own capacity to eventually find himself a wife. There are records that state that Beethoven was very much against marriage, as he was opposed to the weddings of his two younger brothers (ibid., p. 287); although this reaction could be the expression of his own envy: "If I cannot get married, neither should you!"

The first woman to attract his attention in Vienna was Magdalena Willmann, perhaps because, like him, she was from Bonn. She arrived in Vienna in 1794 and Beethoven almost immediately proposed marriage to her, but she rejected him on account of him being, as she put it, "too ugly and half crazy", although it was also possible that he had proposed too soon, without giving her the opportunity to encourage him, as Solomon has suggested (ibid.). There were other women, such as Giulietta Guicciardi, Julie von Vering, Teresa von Brunsvik, Bettina Brentano, Marie Bigot, Teresa Malfatti, and the one considered to be the true "Immortal Beloved", Jozefina Brunsvik. His friend Ries was the first to observe that Beethoven frequently fell in love, but his amorous liaisons never lasted long. Elliot Forbes also remarked that whenever Beethoven faced the possibility of a serious and lasting relationship with a woman, he would very often turn to his music and concentrate on his work. It seems that there was a great ambivalence in Beethoven about establishing a serious bond with a woman, as if a greater percentage of him continuously rejected what another part of him wished so much to achieve.

We can consider several possibilities in trying to understand the meaning of such dissociation: unresolved oedipal conflicts; perhaps as a child having such a close relationship with his mother that later on he was unable to distinguish between her and other women, a condition that often induces ambivalence towards women; desiring those who rejected him and rejecting those who desired him; or being interested in those who were inaccessible either because they were from noble birth, married, or already engaged. It is also possible that he harboured a great amount of hostility towards his mother because she failed to protect him against his father's aggression.

After Beethoven's death in 1827, two love letters signed by him and written passionately to a very special woman were found among his personal possessions; regrettably, they lacked the date and name of the intended recipient. Different scholars have hypothesised about who this woman was; some have considered Giulietta Guicciardi, Therese Malfatti, Amalie Sebald, Antonie Brentano, Anna-Marie Erdödy, sisters Therese von Brunsvik and Josephine Deym, and many others (Tellenbach, 1983). Therese von Brunsvik, who had been a close friend to her sister Josephine, who at one point was considered to be Beethoven's "Immortal Beloved", stated that the "three letters by Beethoven, allegedly to Giulietta ... [c]ould be hoaxes."

If Therese's suspicion was true, we could then think that there was something else that made Beethoven extremely ashamed, to the point of having to cover up, after his own death, the predicament of not being able to establish an intimate relationship with a woman. Unresolved oedipal conditions can often lead to sexual pathology, such as erectile dysfunction or premature ejaculation. In the first line written in his *Tagebuch* (diary), Beethoven said the following: *"You can no longer be a man,* nor for you or for the others." The emphasis was Beethoven's, according to Solomon (p. 235).

CHAPTER FIFTEEN

Freud

Psychoanalysis has been one of the greatest discoveries of the twentieth century, an instrument that teaches people how to use their unconscious for their own benefit, as an organ that always depicts the truth of the individual. Although psychoanalysis is now better understood and more widely used than it was in its beginning, there is still misunderstanding, because different from other doctrines and methodologies, it cannot be understood from books or from theoretical descriptions, since it can only be grasped empirically in the course of our own "therapeutic" experience. "Freud's ideas still remain the property of the few, and a scandal to the most," says Gay (1988, p. 206).

From its very beginning psychoanalysis has been considered an instrument for the resolution of mental pain; however, as Freud himself stated, the main purpose of analysis is to be able to read, and to time, whereabouts we are exactly, mind-wise; the clinical aspects of psychoanalysis are always understand in our unconscious in order to use it as a compass that will allow us to know all the kinds of "side effects". It would be extremely unusual, and suspicious, if someone requested psychoanalytic therapy based only on curiosity about how to use the unconscious in order to improve life. The great majority of those who opt for a psychoanalytic experience have done so based on mental suffering, such as depression or high levels of anxiety.

More than a hundred years since its creation, psychoanalysis is still finding its bearings because, unfortunately, the mind does not give up its secrets very easily. Most of Freud's discoveries will hold true for ever; others, possibly as a consequence of his time, are no longer accurate, while others, in a state of "wild thought", are still waiting for someone—such as Klein, Bion, Meltzer, and many others—to provide them with meaning.

Sigmund Freud was born to a middle class Jewish Galician family on 6 May 1856, in the town of Příbor in Moravia, which was then part of the Austro-Hungarian Empire, but now is known as Freiburg and is part of the Czech Republic. His father, Jacob Freud (1815–1896), married three times and had two children from a previous marriage: Emanuel (1833–1914) and Philip (1836–1911).

After his wife's death he married again at the age of forty, to Amalia Nathansohn (1835–1930) who was twenty years his junior, two years younger than Emanuel and one older than Philip. When Sigmund Freud was born his mother was twenty-one years old and he was already an uncle, because John (1856–1919), Emanuel's older son, who became his childhood playmate, had already been born. Since Amalia was contemporaneous with her younger stepson Philip and he was living with them, they became close friends. "His handsome young mother"—says Gay (1988)—"seemed to him [Freud] far better matched with his half-brother Philip than with his father, yet it was with the father that Amalia Freud shared a bed" (p. 6). It might have been quite confusing for little Freud to see that his "uncle" John, who was more like a brother, called his father Jacob "grandfather"; that his older brothers were old enough to be his father—or uncles—and that his father looked more like a "grandfather". Sigmund Freud, "... the great unriddler of human enigmas, grew up among enough conundrums and confusion to pique the interest of a psychoanalyst" (ibid., p. 4).

In 1859 Jacob left Příbor with his family, which at that time consisted of Amalia, Sigmund, who was three years old, and baby Anna, born in 1858; the second brother, Julius, had died in infancy. They moved first to Leipzig and one year later, in 1860, they were established in Vienna. The older half-brothers, Emanuel and Philip, together with their wives and little John emigrated to England, leaving Sigmund without his playmate companion. Freud, whom his mother had labelled "my golden Sigi", often referred to the special affection his mother displayed towards him. This unconditional love made Freud notice that:

> When you were incontestably the favourite child of your mother, you keep during your lifetime this victor feeling, you keep feeling sure of success, which in reality seldom doesn't fulfil. (Jones, 1961, p. 9)

Gay (ibid.) states that at the time when Freud was a university student,

> [t]he family accepted Freud's boyish imperiousness with equanimity and fostered his sense of being exceptional. If Freud's needs clashed with those of Anna or the others, his prevailed without question. When, intent on his school books, he complained about the noise that Anna's piano lessons were making, the piano vanished never to return … but that sacrifice faded in face of the glorious career they imagined for the studious, lively schoolboy in his cabinet. (p. 14)

Jacob made his living trading in fur, but they were rather poor and while staying in Příbor they rented just one room in a modest house; afterwards, when they moved to Vienna, their financial situation improved. However, the memories of his family's poverty might have been disturbing to Freud, because in a concealed autobiographical note, written in 1899, Freud stated that "he came from well-to-do parents … who lost their fortune after an industrial catastrophe" (ibid., p. 8); possibly an exaggeration representing what he later referred to as "family romance". Obviously, Amalia Freud's fertility, together with the fact that contraceptives did not exist in her time, did not contribute to the family economy; in only six years, four more sisters were born to Freud: Rosa, Marie, Adolfine, and Pauline, together with Alexander the youngest brother. However, this situation was not the greatest tragedy the family had to bear during these years. Gay (ibid.) describes the situation as follows:

> In 1865 and early 1866, the harshness of these years was exacerbated by the indictment, conviction, and imprisonment of Joseph Freud, Jacob's brother, for trading in counterfeit rubbles. This catastrophe was traumatic for the family. Freud did not care for his uncle Joseph, who invaded his dreams, and recalled in the *Interpretation of Dreams*

that the calamity made his father's hair turn grey with grief in a
few days. Probably Jacob Freud's grief was mingled with anxiety:
there is evidence that he and his older sons, who had emigrated to
Manchester, were implicated in Josef Freud's schemes. (p. 8)

After they settled in Vienna their financial situation improved, mostly
from the help they received from the older brothers who had emigrated
to England and were doing well. In 1875, at the time Freud was attend-
ing university, they moved to a six-room apartment, a great difference
from their situation in Freiburg; however, while Freud was assigned one
room the rest of the family, his parents, five sisters, and little brother,
crowded into just three bedrooms.

> Freud alone had his "cabinet" for his private domain, a room
> "long and narrow, with a window looking on the street", more and
> more crammed with books, the adolescent Freud's only luxury. ...
> "Ambitious, outwardly self-assured, brilliant in school and vora-
> cious in his reading ..." "At the Gymnasium," he tersely summed
> up his records, "I was first in my class for seven years, held a privi-
> leged position, was scarcely ever examined." (Ibid., pp. 13, 22)

Around this time, Freud managed to teach himself Spanish and
created a secret society named the "Spanish Academy" formed by "two
members only", he and his classmate Eduard Silberstein. They addressed
each other using names they borrowed from Miguel de Cervantes's
short story: "El Coloquio de los perros" ("Dogs' colloquium")—Cipion for
Freud and Berganza for Silberstein. They communicated using Spanish:
"Queridísimo Berganza" (Dearest Berganza), and in one of the letters
"Cipion" warns "Berganza" that "May no other hand touch this letter"
(Que no otra mano toque esta carta). In another letter Freud expressed his
interest in Gisela Fluss, a girl one year younger than himself, whom he
described as "half-naive, half-cultivated" and accused himself of being
very timid and unable to "give himself the pleasure of conversation
with her". He used another nickname to refer to Gisela: "Ichthysaura"
because "fluss" in German means river and the Ichthyosaurus was
an extinct aquatic dinosaur. There is, however, some confusion about
Freud's infatuation with this girl, as it is not clear if it was directed
towards Gisela or her mother, Frau Fluss, to whom he dedicated a series
of charming accolades: "her intelligence, cultivation, versatility, cheer-
fulness, cordiality, and hospitality", and so on.

It seems he acknowledged, intuitively anticipating the kind of perception to which he would devote his life, "that I have transferred respect for the mother to friendship for the daughter". (Ibid., pp. 22–23)

Originally, under pressure from an older gymnasium colleague, Freud was planning to enter the faculty of law; however, influenced by the work of Darwin, relevant at that time, as well as by Goethe's essay "On Nature", presented at a popular conference by Professor Carl Brühl, "shortly before my final examinations, I decided to inscribe myself in medicine" (Gay, ibid., p. 24). There is a common itinerary psychoanalysts usually follow: from medicine to psychiatry and finally to psychoanalytic training. In 1935 Freud stated that he had followed a "lifelong detour through the natural sciences, medicine and psychotherapy", the difference being, however, that in the case of psychoanalysts today, thanks to Freud, we do not have to invent psychoanalysis! What exactly is the unconscious factor that encourages this familiar journey? In 1875, in the second year of medical school, Freud wrote to his friend "Berganza":

"I now have more than one ideal. To the theoretical one of my earlier years a practical one has now been added. Last year, asked what my greatest wish might be, I would have answered a laboratory and free time, or a ship on the ocean with all the instruments the researcher needs … Now I vacillate about whether I should not rather say: a large hospital and plenty of money, to curtail some of the evils which befall our bodies, or remove them from the world." (Ibid., p. 26)

And in 1927 "he insisted that he had never properly been a physician and had found his way back to his real vocation after an extended and circuitous journey" (ibid., p. 27).

"The various branches of medicine proper, apart from psychiatry, had no attraction for me," said Freud (1925, p. 2) in his autobiography. Under the guidance of Ernst Brücke he started work at a physiology laboratory for neurological investigations. Possibly pressured by the need to understand the inner nature of his patients' suffering, in the autumn of 1885 Freud obtained a travelling bursary and journeyed to Paris to attend Charcot's lectures, which were in fashion at the time, where he learned about the use of hypnosis to treat hysterical patients.

In 1886 he resigned his hospital post and entered private practice specialising in "nervous disorders", a specialty then in its very beginning. What he discovered at this time—among many other things—was first that hysterical paralysis was not the consequence of a neurological localisation, as many believed, but carried a specific *meaning* that remained repressed; second, that all of his patients' symptomatology was related to repressed sexual matters. This perception, however, was time-related and culturally related, in a similar way to the description made by anatomists of the existence of a vertical fold on the frontal face of women's liver, which was later understood as a consequence of the use of corsets. At that time, sexuality was not the open subject it is today. Finally, the awareness that we could treat our own mental life "as one had always treated other people's … what held good for other people must be applicable to oneself" (ibid., p. 15); a concept that became a corner-stone in psychoanalytic training.

Freud's journey from medicine to neurophysiology and later to the discovery of the unconscious, of the dialectical topography of the mind, defence mechanisms, narcissism, and many other mental constructs, was possibly a consequence of Freud's relentless search for the truth, probably impelled by what Grotstein (2004) referred to as a "truth drive", in addition to a narcissistic need—in a healthy sense—of searching for awareness of his own pre-conceptual trauma, to treat himself "as one had always treated other people".

In 1886 he married Martha Bernays (1861–1951), the granddaughter of Isaac Bernays, a chief rabbi in Hamburg, and had six children: Mathilde (1887–1978), Jean-Martin Freud (1889–1967), Oliver Freud (1891–1969), Ernst Freud (1892–1970), Sophie Freud (1893–1920), and Anna Freud (1895–1982).

CHAPTER SIXTEEN

Einstein

Hoffmann (1972) has, with justice, observed that there is an unusual paradox about Einstein: he became a living legend, "a veritable folk hero, looked upon as an oracle, entertained by royalty, statesmen, and other celebrities, and treated by the public and press as if he were a movie star rather than a scientist" (p. 3); however, if you were to ask any of his admirers why he was so famous, most of them would not be able to provide a meaningful answer. "The most incomprehensible thing about the world," said Einstein, "is that it is comprehensible" (Einstein, 1954, p. 292). Even though quantum theory was evolving at that time, no other well-known physicist—such as Werner Heisenberg or Niels Böhr—received such public recognition. Something else to admire about him was how in spite of all this fame he never changed his humility, simplicity, and sense of humour. Hoffmann states that:

> When a passenger on a train, not recognizing him, asked him his occupation, he ruefully replied, "I am an artists' model." Harassed by requests for his autograph, he remarked to friends that autograph hunting was the last vestige of cannibalism: people used to eat people, but now they sought symbolic pieces of them instead. (p. 4)

Einstein became well-known not only because of what he said but also when he said it. In 1905, when he produced his theory of relativity, he was only twenty-six years old, while the other renowned physicists were much older, such as Max Planck who was forty-seven, Hendrick Lorentz fifty-two, Henri Poincaré fifty-one, and Marie Curie thirty-eighty, just to mention the better-known.

Einstein was born in Ulm, Germany on 14 March 1879 and died on 18 April 1955, in Princeton, New Jersey, US. His parents were Hermann Einstein (1847–1902) a salesman and engineer, and Pauline Koch (1858–1920), who were, like Freud's family, non-observant Jews. Einstein was the elder child and had a sister, Maja Einstein (1881–1951), two years his junior. He was a peculiar child; he was disproportionately gifted with a visual inclination at the expense of his verbal skills. He did not learn to talk until the age of three, but instead he favoured nonverbal activities that involved the use of his visual abilities. In 1945 Einstein recalled this situation in a letter: "My parents were worried because I started to talk comparatively late, and they consulted the doctor because of it … I was … certainly not younger than three" (ibid., p. 14). There is however, some contradiction, because in a letter written by his grand-mother on 24 June 1881, when he was two years and three months old, she said: "We have fond recollections of little Albert. He was so dear and good, and we talk again and again of his droll ideas" (ibid., p. 13). What the true meaning of "droll" from the point of view of a grandmother could be, we will never know.

In 1884 he received private education in order to prepare for school, and a year later he started to learn to play the violin. Beginning in 1885 he received his primary education at a Catholic school in Munich (Petersschule). He first realised the wonders of science at the age of four or five, when his father introduced him to the great mystery of the earth's magnetic field by giving him a compass as a present while he was ill. Einstein later said: "I can still remember—or at least I believe I can remember—that this experience made a deep and lasting impression on me" (ibid., p. 9). Later in his life, although still a child, Einstein's uncle, Jacob, introduced him to mathematics, specifically equations.

In 1880 the family moved from Ulm to Munich where his father and his uncle Jacob created the "Elektrotechnische Fabrik J. Einstein & Cie", a company that manufactured electrical parts and provided direct current. When "direct current" was taken over by "alternating current", the business failed, and in 1894, searching for better possibilities, the family moved to Milan and then to Pavia, while Einstein, who was then fifteen years old, stayed behind. He was considered rebellious against authority and in a letter written by him at this time he said:

> When I was in the seventh grade at the Luitpold Gymnasium, I was summoned by my home-room teacher [the Greek teacher, who like Freud's father, felt that Albert would never amount to anything] who expressed the wish that I leave the school. To my remark that I had done nothing amiss he replied only "your mere presence spoils the respect of the class for me". (Ibid., p. 25)

His resentment was so great that he decided to give up his German citizenship, and later, in 1933, he wrote about these difficult times:

> The over-emphasized military mentality in the German State was alien to me even as a boy. When my father moved to Italy he took steps, at my request, to have me released from German citizenship because I wanted to become a Swiss citizen. (Ibid., p. 26)

There is also a letter from a friend who wrote to Albert about an incident he heard about from his uncle Jacob:

> Your uncle ... had told me that he had great difficulty with some calculations for the construction of some machine. Some days later ... he said, "You know, it is really fabulous with my nephew. After I and my assistant-engineer had been racking our brains for days, that young sprig had got the whole thing in scarcely fifteen minutes. You will hear of him yet." (Ibid.)

Within a year, still without having completed secondary school, Einstein failed an entrance examination that would have allowed him to pursue a course of study leading to a diploma as an electrical engineer at the Swiss Federal Institute of Technology. He spent the next year in nearby Aarau at the cantonal secondary school, where he enjoyed excellent teachers and first-rate facilities in physics. Einstein returned in 1896 to the Swiss Federal Institute of Technology, where he graduated in 1900, as a secondary school teacher of mathematics and physics. At the time when he failed his entrance examination, one of his teachers, professor of physics Heinrich Weber, aware of Einstein's potential, offered him the opportunity to attend his lectures; this gracious offer, however, changed drastically, possibly as a result of Einstein's taciturn and rebel-lious stance. The same Weber, who went out of his way to help, said to him: "You're a clever fellow! But you have one fault. You won't let any-one tell you a thing. You won't let anyone tell you a thing" (ibid., p. 32). This remark later became a critical impediment to finding a position at the university, and in 1901, Einstein wrote:

> From what people tell me, I am not in the good graces of any of my former teachers … I would long ago have found [a position in a university] had not Weber intrigued against me. (Ibid.)

There were agonising times of being penniless and not able to find a job; his father even wrote a letter to Wilhelm Oswald, professor of physics at the University of Leipzig, pleading for help, without result. It was, once again, his personal friend Marcel Grossmann who, in 1902, helped him to find a position at the Swiss Patent Office in Bern. In 1903 he married Mileva Maric (1875–1948), a Serbian physicist, Greek Orthodox, and classmate at the Zurich Polytechnic. A year later their first son, Hans Albert (1904–1973), was born and their second, Eduard, in 1910, who twenty years later had a breakdown, was diagnosed as schizophrenic, and remained secluded in a mental hospital until his death in 1950. Einstein's total commitment to his creative work interfered with his duties as husband and father, a situation that became more complicated after 1905, his "miracle year".

Due to mutual disagreement, Mileva and Einstein were separated in 1914, and finally divorced in March 1919. Three and a half months later, Einstein married his first cousin Elsa (1876–1936) who had divorced a textile trader from Berlin, Max Löwenthal, and had two daughters, Ilse (1897–1934) and Margot (1900–1986). Einstein and Elsa, who had known each other since childhood, started a relationship at Easter 1912, while he was still married to Mileva. There were problems between them, too, because as Einstein became more famous, women were attracted to him, and he usually flirted with them. Elsa died in 1936 after they had moved to the United States, possibly from high blood pressure. Einstein was very close to Ilse and Margot, his stepdaughters; Ilse was his secretary until 1924 when she married Rudolf Kayser, a German editor. After Hitler took power in 1933, Rudolf and Ilse moved to the Netherlands and afterwards to Paris where she died in 1934. Margot married Dimitri Marianoff, who was an assistant to Einstein, and they were divorced seven years later. In 1934 she moved to Princeton in the US with her parents, became a sculptor, and stayed there until her death in 1986. Since she outlived the rest of Einstein's immediate family, she became the executor of her famous stepfather's will. When she bestowed his correspondence of 1300 letters to the Hebrew University in Jerusalem, she demanded that they not be published until twenty years after her death. They were opened in 2006 and described some of Einstein's affairs, of how he was honest and rather open about this "wrong-doing", and that he was a more conscientious father and husband than he was believed to be.

From 1902 to 1905, Einstein published several papers in the *Annalen der Physik*, which dealt with thermodynamics and entropy, asserting the impossibility of fabricating perpetual motion machines, an interest perhaps inspired by projects presented to the Patent Office. In 1905, when he published his theory of special relativity, Einstein was only twenty-six years old. He based his findings on discoveries made by Maxwell between 1861 and 1864, who declared that light waves and electromagnetic waves are in essence the same thing, and also on Max Planck's 1900 contributions on black-body radiation, which, he had observed, was not produced smoothly but in jumps of discrete amounts he referred to as *quanta*.

The main problem astrophysics faced at that time was that velocity is relative and that there is not an absolute motion. An object might appear static, but the earth is orbiting the sun at 57,000 kilometres per hour, whilst the sun is also moving with its planets through the galaxy. Only light, as a form of radiation consisting of particles, is constant and moving at the speed of 300,000 kilometres per second. Before Einstein it was believed that the entire universe was filled with a fixed and invisible substance, called "ether", that carried the light waves, something Einstein completely denied; as a result, there was no meaning to the notion of absolute length and time. In the special theory of relativity, the speed of light becomes an absolute, because regardless of how quickly a source of light or the observer move, the speed of light relative to the observer is always the same: 300,000 kilometres per second.

The general theory of relativity, produced in 1916, considered the subject of gravity, the fact that matter does not merely draw other matter to it in empty space, as Newton made us believe, but rather that matter distorts the space-time dimension and it is such distortion that affects matter. There is a sort of circularity in the sense that the distribution of matter and energy is controlled by the curvature of space, and this geometry determines the motion of matter and energy. Considering light as formed by particles implies that light has a mass and, in consequence, is affected by gravity, meaning that it is attracted by a large body such as the sun. In 1919 British astronomer Arthur Eddington photographed the solar eclipse off the west coast of Africa to test Einstein's observation, as a result of which the general theory of relativity became widely accepted. In 1921, Einstein was awarded the Nobel Prize for physics and has since become most famous for his equation showing the relationship between mass and energy: $E=MC^2$, which means that if we were to deconstruct a molecule of water made of two atoms of hydrogen and one of oxygen, the energy produced would be equal to the mass of the molecule plus the speed of light multiplied by itself; or, in other words, an unbelievable amount of energy would be released. The equation was published in 1905 as part of the special theory of relativity in a three-page paper: "Does the inertia of a body depend on its energy content?" The road to atomic energy was established.

CHAPTER SEVENTEEN

Gandhi

I don't have anything new to teach the world. The truth and the nonviolence are as old as the mountains.

—Gandhi

Gandhi is "the Great Soul in beggar's garb"

—Tagore

It is not easy to understand the incongruities in Gandhi's story—his evident sense of frailty, his paralysing phobias and "shyness", and at the same time, his capacity to achieve what he did without ever commanding an army or firing a single shot. In spite of his emotional limitations, he was able to liberate his country from the iron grip of the mighty British Empire that dominated India for almost a century (1858–1947). What were his psychological resources and from where did he derive his ability to achieve what appears an insurmountable task?

Mohandas Karamchand Gandhi (Moniya, Bapu) (1869–1948) was born on 2 October 1869, in the port city of Porbandar on the Kathiawar Peninsula on the shores of the Arabian Sea. He was the youngest son of Karamchand Gandhi (1822–1885) and Putlibai Gandhi (1844–1891). His mother was twenty-five years old when he was born, and is described as the ideal housewife (Erikson, 1969, p. 105); Kaba, his father, who was forty-seven years old, came from a well-known and respected provincial family, who for generations had occupied ministerial positions in Kathiawar Peninsula. Kaba married four times and had four daughters from the first and second marriages; with Putlibai, his last wife, he had an older son, Laxmidas (1860–1914), a daughter: Raliatbehn (1862–1960), and three boys, Gandhi being the youngest. Six generations of Gandhis were ministers and, in some states, prime ministers: "The 'sovereignty' of these states," says Erikson (1969),

> ... fostered by the British as long as it suited their policies, helped to preserve a certain regional, feudal, and professional pride which—in all its precariousness—would be of great importance to Gandhi's original world-image. (p. 104)

Referring to his father, Gandhi asserts in his autobiography:

> ... To a certain extent he might have been given to carnal pleasures ... My father never had any ambition to accumulate riches and left us very little property. He had no education, save that of experience ... He was a lover of his clan, truthful, brave and generous, but short-tempered. (Gandhi, 1957, pp. 3–4)

And about his mother he says:

> The outstanding impression my mother has left on my memory is that of saintliness. She was deeply religious. (Ibid.)

Erikson (1969), on the other hand, describes the child Gandhi as follows:

> ... big and protruding ears which help to "round out" the little boy's face but later rob the Mahatma's countenance of its proportions, especially when he laughed in his toothless way. That all his life he loved to laugh and make others laugh ... he would write in his diary that *he could always console his mother by making her laugh heartily*. (p. 103, our emphasis)

Gandhi grew up being the little one in a big house with many small rooms crowded with people from a very large family, where his parents and siblings, as well as his father's five brothers and their own families, shared the same lodgings. The largest room in the house was reserved for his father who acted as the head of the clan and was also prime minister of the city in which they were living. According to Gandhi (1957), his father was incorruptible and had earned a name for himself as being strictly impartial in his family as well as outside of it. Being the last child of a young mother and an ageing father gave Gandhi a privileged position in the family and one exposed to being spoilt. This situation, suggests Erikson (ibid.)

> ... seems to have cultivated this advantage in developing that quality of tenacious and clever attachment which made his parents feel that their relationship to him was a unique one and made him in turn, feel that his was the fate of an elect being. (p. 106)

As a child he was considered extremely curious and restless:

> Gandhi's enormous perambulatory vigour in later years is well known ... [it] imposed quite a job on those who were supposed to keep an eye on him while his mother was busy. His older sister seems to have been the chosen victim. When she was ninety, this sister described Moniya [Gandhi] as "restless as mercury" and "full of curiosity." (Ibid., p. 107)

Erikson quotes Gandhi's confession to Pyarelal, his secretary:

> I was my mother's pet child, first because I was the smallest of her children but also because there was nothing dearer to my heart than her service. My brothers were fond of play and frolic. I found not much in common with them. I had no close bond with my sister either. Play had absolutely no fascination for me in preference to my mother's service. Whenever she wanted me for anything, I ran to her. (Erikson, ibid., p. 110)

We can recall what Freud said about this kind of relationship, when a child becomes his mother's favourite:

> When you were incontestably the favourite child of your mother, you keep during your lifetime this victor feeling, you keep feeling sure of success, which in reality seldom doesn't fulfil. (Jones, 1961, p. 9)

At the same time there is also the possibility that being the youngest child can induce a sense of impotence and insignificance in relation to the rest of his siblings, a condition that very often provokes the need to compensate for such impotence by using mechanisms of "reaction formation", meaning being able to help himself by using opposite means, such as whatever he senses is a form of "overachievement". We have previously stated in relation to this aspect (López-Corvo, 2014, p. 125), how the youngest child in a large family compensates the feeling of insignificance with opposite emotions, such as idealisation and feelings of significance. We will come back to this later on.

Overprotection on the other hand, is a form of child abuse, and can induce feelings of inadequacy, fears, or phobias. Gandhi recalls childhood fears that he attributed to being a vegetarian:

> ... I was a coward. I used to be haunted by the fear of thieves, ghosts, and serpents. I did not dare to stir out of doors at night. Darkness was a terror to me. It was almost impossible for me to sleep in the dark, as I would imagine ghosts coming from one direction, thieves from another and serpents from a third. I could not therefore bear to sleep without a light in the room. (Gandhi, 1957, ibid., p. 20)

Gandhi refers to his father as someone who did not harbour great pretension, and it has been recorded, for instance, how he helped his wife with housework:

> ... It was a familiar sight, which the people of Porbandar still remember, of him sitting in the Shrinathji temple day after day, peeling and paring the vegetables for his wife's kitchen, while he discussed with his visitors and officials affairs of the State. (Gandhi, 1958–1994, CWMG, XIV, p. 286)

We can wonder if these roles, acted out by both parents, might have been confusing for the child Gandhi's own process of identification; of finding difficultly in discriminating between what was masculine and what was feminine:

> ... Some such latent element [homosexuality] cannot be excluded, especially in view of Mohandas's passionate relationship to all his single counter players to whom he gave more of himself than

he could afford and from whom he wanted he knew not what. (Erikson, ibid., p. 137)

The Gandhis were religious people, devoted to Jainism in Hinduism, which strongly believes in many forms of abstinence, such as of sex, alcohol, and the consumption of meat. "The opposition to and abhorrence of meat-eating," says Gandhi (1957)

> ... that existed ... among the Jains and Vaishanavas were to be seen nowhere else in India or outside in such strength. These were the traditions in which I was born and bred. And I was extremely devoted to my parents. I knew that the moment they came to know of my having eaten meat they would be shocked to death. (p. 21)·

Something often observed in vegetarian patients is fear of oedipal aggression, about their own unconscious fantasy of murdering and cannibalising their parents, so they resort to becoming vegetarians in order to avoid finding the spoils of their supposed murder in what they eat. In other words, they fear acting out their cannibalistic fantasies. This is also why it is so repugnant to consume domestic animals, such as dogs, horses, cats, and so on, because these animals are too close to humans.

Mohandas Gandhi married in 1883, at the age of thirteen, Kasturba (1869–1944), a girl of the same age, in the Indian style of a pre-arrangement based on convenience and economy made by their parents when they were still infants. Gandhi describes it as follows:

> It was only through these preparations that we got warning of the coming event. I do not think it meant to me anything more than the prospect of good clothes to wear, drum beating, marriage processions, rich dinners and a strange girl to play with. The carnal desire came later. (Gandhi, 1957, p. 9)

Gandhi had four sons with his wife Kasturba: Harilal (1888–1948), Manilal (1892–1956), Ramdas (1897–1969), and Devdas (1900–1957). At the age of eighteen, exactly a year after his first son was born, Mohandas left for England to pursue a degree in law. However, he was required to obtain permission from his older family members, mainly his mother, as well as people from his caste, who were strongly against it, as they all feared he would be disloyal to his religion and his abstinence of sex and food. But he was determined and finally able to get his own way.

Gandhi's "Tragedy"

In his autobiography Gandhi provides two chapters on a situation he referred to as "a tragedy", where he describes his friendship with Sheik Mehtab, a classmate from high school, his senior and previously his brother Karsandas' friend (Weber, 2004, p. 22). Apparently, he protected Gandhi from being bullied at school since he often "told on others in the name of truth" (Erikson, ibid., p. 134). Why was Mehtab a tragedy for Gandhi? He was the first Muslim friend Gandhi had with a significant emotional influence on him, persuaded him to break his vegetarian diet and fall into the sinful acts of eating meat and being unfaithful to his wife. There was a general belief in India that they were ruled by the British because the British were powerful and strong as a result of being meat eaters. Gandhi (1957, p. 21) quotes the following rhyme:

> Behold the mighty Englishman
> He rules the Indian small,
> Because being a meat-eater
> He is five cubits tall.

Gandhi also states that he became Mehtab's friend with the idea of reforming him, but later realised that his means were mistaken, because "a reformer cannot have close intimacy with whom he seeks to reform". However, it seems that this belief that he could reform his friend was an excuse to conceal the opposite, that is, his admiration for Mehtab's daring. "By all accounts," said Weber (ibid.), "he was handsome, outgoing, fearless and a star athlete—everything that Gandhi was not" (ibid.). Possibly, as Erikson (ibid., p. 134) suggests, Mehtab represented an instrument of freedom to Gandhi, by which he might liberate himself from his fears, hesitations, and dependency on his wife and his parents. As he states, to achieve such state of independence he would need to "murder" his parents, meaning that he would have to wait until they died:

> Though it is essential to eat meat, and also essential to take up food "reform" in the country, yet deceiving and lying to one's father and

mother is worse than not eating meat. In their lifetime, therefore, meat-eating must be out of the question. *When they are no more and I have found my freedom*, I will eat meat openly … (Gandhi, ibid., p. 23, our emphasis)

Erikson also adds that it was quite possible Gandhi used this friendship as a container in which to project his own "personal devil" in order to make Mehtab the personification of his own "negative identity". Gandhi was advised about his friend's bad influence, as all of his family strongly disliked him. Erikson suggested that Mehtab "would have had to be invented if he had not existed". He was "… everything in himself which he tried to isolate and subdue and which yet was part of him" (ibid., p. 135).

We believe there is a significant poignant ambivalence in Gandhi between his powerful emotional ties to his parents, mostly to his mother, and his desire to achieve total freedom without any form of dependency; however, like most adolescents, his dependency might have produced anger, while his attempts for freedom generated guilt, a condition that in its compulsive repetition acts as a trap. Perhaps Mohandas unconsciously felt that his marriage was going to liberate him from his emotional dependency on his parents; however, according to him, it became a more powerful addiction in the form of sexual desire. Mehtab convinced Gandhi to be disloyal to his spouse and effectively persuaded him, by paying for him, to visit a brothel, but Gandhi's anxiety was so great that he became impotent and the prostitute "naturally lost patience with me, and showed me the door, with abuses and insults" (Gandhi, ibid., p. 17). While in London, Gandhi used to write to Kasturba, his illiterate wife, addressing his correspondence to Mehtab—whom Kasturba strongly despised—and asked him to read Gandhi's letters to Kasturba, a situation that gave rise to such a state of desperation that she threatened to leave him. Later, at the time he wrote his autobiography, he intensely repented of this behaviour.

There is literature about the unconscious reasons that moved Mohandas to become a friend of Mehtab, but there is little about what motivated the latter to form an intense emotional link with Gandhi. Erikson (ibid., p. 134) and Weber (ibid., p. 23) suggest there could have been some form of adolescent complicity between them about fear of heterosexual relationships, some homoerotic mockery of masculinity that youths often act out in order to deal with their own feminine identifications. But we can also consider another possibility, the existence of a significant amount of envy in Mehtab towards the "goodness" (Bion, 1965; Klein, 1952) Gandhi continuously flaunted, as well as a perverse need to foster a complicity with him in order to destroy that goodness: if he was unfaithful or broke his promise and ate meat or drank alcohol, there was then nothing to envy and to feel bad about; Gandhi was, after all, as dreadful as he was. Mehtab would do anything for Gandhi, but Gandhi would eventually help him to find out that goodness did not exist! Gandhi learnt this lesson late; he was already living in South Africa, when he sent for Mehab to help him with his domestic arrangements. As soon as he arrived he enviously undermined a law clerk who was living in the household, possibly because he felt he was too close to Gandhi, and finally convinced Gandhi that the clerk had been dishonest and that he should be discharged. The clerk "left heart-broken" and afterwards, when Gandhi discovered the truth about Mehab, he tried to compensate for the blunder, but the clerk refused to forgive him. Sometime later, after finding that Mehab had brought a prostitute into the house, he finally broke off his friendship with him.

Becoming a lawyer in London

Gandhi's family recognised from very early on that, since he had obtained a better education than the rest of his brothers, he was the best candidate to go to London and to become a barrister, and then be able, later on, to succeed his uncle and his father as the Diwan or leader; this was a consideration that was supported by a Brahmin priest and other individuals close to the family. Gandhi left for England on 4 September 1888 and arrived in London on 29 October.

A concern that haunted Gandhi while in England was the promise made to his mother that he would seriously abstain from meat, alcohol, and women. At the beginning he felt emotionally overwhelmed by his separation from his mother, something that would be considered somewhat unusual in Western culture because he was then eighteen years old. In his autobiography he says:

> My mother's love always haunted me. At night the tears would stream down my cheeks ... It was impossible to share my misery

with anyone ... Everything was strange—the people, their ways,
and even their dwellings. (1957, pp. 44–45)

He began studying law, registered at the "Inner Temple", one of the
professional associations in London for barristers and judges, and lived
with an Anglo-Indian family. The landlady had great difficulties providing him with a vegetarian diet, which was usually too bland and
always left him hungry, until he found a vegetarian restaurant in town.
He joined the Vegetarian Society and even became part of the executive
committee. He changed his Indian way of dressing to the British style,
tried to play violin, studied elocution, and learned to dance, something
he gave up once he realised that this was "a stage of indulgence" that he
conveniently changed into a more modest way of living (ibid., p. 52).

Gandhi was called to the bar on 10 June 1891, enrolled in the High
Court of London on the 11 June, and left for India the next day. About
this time he has this to say:

> But notwithstanding my study there was no end to my help-
> lessness and fear. I did not feel myself qualified to practice law.
> (Ibid., p. 80)

He reached Bombay on 6 July. On arriving he learned the of his
mother's passing away, which his family had decided not to communicate. He decided to practice law in Bombay but had difficulties in cross-
questioning witnesses:

> I stood up, but my heart sank into my boots. My head was reel-
> ing and I felt as though the whole court was doing likewise.
> I could think of no question to ask. The judge must have laughed.
> (Ibid. p. 94)

South Africa and India: learning from experience

Unable to support himself in Bombay, he returned to Rajkot, where he
stayed for a short while working with his brother, until he had a disagreement with a British officer, and, in April 1893, after receiving an
offer from a large law firm in South Africa, he decided to leave India.
He stayed in South Africa until May 1896, when he took a six-month
break and went to India to see his family.

He was twenty-four years old when he started work in the city of Pretoria as a legal representative for the Muslim Indian Traders. In total, he stayed in South Africa for twenty-one years, where he learned to provide assistance to the impoverished, indentured labourers who had very limited rights, regardless of nationality, as well as to practice *ahimsa*, or the principle of nonviolence, and *Satyagraha*, or devotion to the truth (ibid., pp. 318–319). "I have no doubt that the British Government is a powerful Government, but I have no doubt also that Satyagraha is a sovereign remedy," he said at the time (ibid., p. 380). His experience made him aware of how unfairly the rich and powerful treated the poor and helpless, and also, in the long term, introduced him to politics and determined his future endeavour of freeing his country from British domination. In 1994, the year black people obtained the right to vote in South Africa, Gandhi was proclaimed a national hero and many monuments and streets with his name were created.

On his way to Pretoria in May 1903, he was forced to leave the first-class train carriage for which he had bought a ticket because he was coloured, and forced to sit with the driver. Very angry about this incident, he wrote a telegram to the general manager of the railway. Insisting, as he did, on travelling first class, even after having been beaten and threatened, illustrates how extremely persistent and determined he was.

In his autobiography, Gandhi seldom talks about his wife and children. In December 1896, returning by boat to South Africa with his wife and two older children, they went through a powerful storm, and most of the passengers believed they were going to capsize and drown. After arrival they were held in quarantine for twenty-three days, because of the outbreak of plague in India. While disembarking, Gandhi was attacked by a mob of white settlers who almost killed him and later surrounded his house with his wife and children inside. Gandhi had to escape in disguise to a police station, where he was kept for three days for his own protection. However, he refused to press charges against any member of the mob, stating it was one of his principles not to seek redress for a personal wrong in a court of law.

However, describing these ordeals, Gandhi never mentions how his wife and small children felt about being in such terrifying situations. Being so often absent from his family and for such long periods of time could have been for several reasons: i) his own duties and work; ii) psychological motives stemming from his own pre-conceptual trauma that induced the unconscious demand to compensate for the experience of being the "little one in a large household", together with the possibility of having identified with his own busy and absent father who was a politician and civil servant; and iii) because in his culture men's duties were considered to be more important than the family's welfare.

Harilal Gandhi

Harilal was Gandhi's eldest son, who presented serious forms of acting out, such as alcoholism, public drunkenness, delinquent behaviour, debauchery, and getting a police record. This was perhaps a result of his father's political career. The same year Harilal was born, Gandhi left for London, where he stayed for the next three years. In 1891 Gandhi came back to India and stayed until 1893, when he left again for South Africa until 1896. At this time, he again returned to India to collect his wife and children and to settle in South Africa for the next eighteen years, when, in December 1914, at the break of the First World War, he returned to his country. As we can see, Gandhi was away during the first years of Harilal's life, a significant time in the structuring of a child's personality. Our mother provides us with unconditional love; our father, who rescues us from our mother's symbiotic power, provides us with hope and freedom. A child that grows up without a father faces the possibility of becoming a child from the claustrum, as stated by Meltzer (1992),[1] becoming trapped in his mother's unconscious mental spaces, four of which Meltzer describes as the head, the breast, the vagina, and the anus; the last being related to addictions, as in the case of Harilal. We can also add that this kind of rebellion, often observed in adolescents, contains a type of self-envy mechanism, where out of intense anger and a narcissistic confusion, adolescents resort to an attack on themselves, on the child they feel their parents wish them to become. At one point, Gandhi stated that his son's wrong-doings were possibly his own fault, because he felt at the time of his conception a "slave of his passions", meaning perhaps that he felt his son's conflicts were related to Gandhi's sexual vehemence.

It has been said that Harilal wished to go to England to follow in his father's footsteps and become a barrister, but Gandhi was strongly opposed to this, because he believed allowing his son a Western form of education was in conflict with his attempt to liberate India from the British. In 1911, when he was twenty-three years old, Harilal renounced all of his family ties, possibly out of great resentment, frustration, and helplessness; later, for similar reasons and a sense of powerlessness in the face of his powerful father, and perhaps to provoke him, he converted to Islam. On 15 May 2014, a letter written by Gandhi in June 1935 to his eldest son Harilal, was auctioned in London by Mullock's, where he appears to refer to a conversation he had with his granddaughter Manu, Harilal's daughter, who had come to stay with Gandhi at Sabarmati Ashram in Gujarat:

> "Manu is telling me a number of dangerous things about you. She says that you had raped her even before she was eight years and she was so much hurt that medical treatment was also to be taken."
> (Press Trust of India, London, 2014)

However, there are others who argue that the content of this letter has been taken out of context, because Gandhi, they say, was referring to Harilal's sister-in-law, the sister of his deceased wife who was a child widow, and not to his daughter. Harilal died in June 1948, from cirrhosis of the liver caused by his alcoholism, in a municipal hospital in Mumbai, shortly after his father was fatally shot.[2]

His experiment with "brahmacharya" or sexual abstinence

In his thirties Gandhi started to abstain from sexual relations with his wife: "The very first change I made in my mode of life was to stop sharing the same bed with my wife or seeking privacy with her" (Gandhi, 1958–1994, vol. 2, p. 152). It is important to recognise that Gandhi often associated fasting with sexuality, and in his autobiography (1957), for instance, he writes that, "Fasting can help to cure animal passion, only if it is undertaken with a view to self-restraint" (p. 330). And also:

> We are not really in earnest about getting this disease of sexual desire cured. We are not willing to sacrifice our all for it ... we should give up everything that gives rise to desire. The question of diet also deserves consideration in this connection. That is a virgin field. (Ibid., vol. 32, p. 135)
> ... One cannot hope to observe *brahmacharya* while one resorts to a diet that stimulates the sexual urge. (1958–1994, vol. 40, p. 67)

Gandhi (1964) took a vow of total sexual abstinence or *brahmacharya* in 1906 when he was thirty-eight years old. He started his experiment by sleeping naked with naked young girls. According to him, it was an attempt to test his will power by proving to himself that he would not respond to any form of sexual stimulation. He started with Sushila Nayar, his beautiful personal physician, also sister to his own secretary, who was later replaced by Manu, his eighteen-year-old grandniece. Masson (1974) refers to a letter Gandhi wrote to Satish Chandra Mukherji about his grandniece:

> "A young girl (19) who is in the place of granddaughter to me by relation shares the same bed with me, not for any animal satisfaction but for (to me) valid moral reasons. She claims to be free from the passion that a girl of her age generally has and I claim to be a practised *brahmachari*. Do you see anything bad or unjustifiable in this juxtaposition?"

Mason concludes:

> At the very least one can say that here was a man seriously disturbed seemingly requesting, albeit belatedly, some kind of help. (p. 520).

After his wife's death, he had more women around him and demanded that many of them sleep with him, while at the same time he advised them not to sleep with their own husbands. Eventually, the reasons for his experiment shifted from spiritual to political, and as India approached independence, Gandhi described his sexual experiments, feeling that it was of national importance, as he stated that the true service of the country demanded his observance. He acted as he wished, and if questioned, he turned his own desires into a powerful plan of universal benefit. Gandhi made up the rules as he went along. However, as he became bolder in his gratifications, his behaviour was generally discussed and strongly criticised by family, friends, and well-known politicians; several members of his staff resigned and newspapers refused to print Gandhi's discussions on his sleeping arrangements.

It is possible that Gandhi was genuinely honest when he followed his own beliefs and experimented by acting on them; the real difficulty, however, was to ignore the impact that such decisions had on others;

such as the amount of guilt provoked in his own children's minds—fuelled by their own omnipotence—when he opted to use fasting to deal with whatever he considered was his children's misbehaviour, and the amount of guilt he could have stimulated in them as a result of him suffering and even dying as he did.

Gandhi's revolution

Gandhi said: "without infinite patience it was impossible to get the people to do any work. It is the reformer who is anxious for the reform, from which he should expect nothing better than opposition, abhorrence and even mortal persecution" (Gandhi, 1957, p. 218). In his first public appearance in India, during the opening ceremony for the Banaras Hindu University in February 1916, addressing his audience in English, Gandhi astounded them when he said that he felt "deeply humiliated and shamed", for being required "to address my countrymen in a language that is foreign to me". And, shocking them even further, he said "to the bejewelled princes: There is no salvation for India unless you strip yourselves of this jewellery and hold it in trust for your countrymen in India" (ibid.). Many princes walked out!

Gandhi's peaceful revolution was a slow process that took many years to get established. It was the result of a number of complex variables, such as Gandhi's own idiosyncrasy, the Indian culture and traditions as well as the British take-over, structuring, and organisation of what is today India and Pakistan. It was a domination so effectively administered that Indians did not resist but peacefully surrendered for almost a century to the "civilised" alien ruler. In 1899, during the Boer war in South Africa between British and the Boers (Dutch settlers), although Gandhi's sympathy was for the latter who were fighting for independence, he advised his followers to support the British because he believed they were British subjects, and it was their duty to defend the Empire when it was threatened. He therefore organised and trained an Indian Ambulance Corps to help the injured. Nineteen years later, during the First World War, while in England, he again made the same statement.

The British had settled in India around the 1600s as a private non-governmental company, established by wealthy merchants and aristocrats with the purpose of creating a commercial exchange with East India and China, under the name of the Honourable East India

Company (EIC). It traded basic commodities such as cotton, silk, indigo dye, salt, tea, and opium, and, in due course, accounted for half of global trade, with its own private army, implementing military power and administrative functions. The company ruled most of India after the Battle of Plassey in 1757, until the *sepoys'* (Indian soldiers) revolution in 1857, which was considered the first war of independence. It was this war that induced the British Crown to take over from the company and to assume direct control of India by becoming the British Raj that ruled India for a century.

Gandhi learned from experience by observing the results of his actions, primarily in South Africa and later on in his own country. He says that he discovered after his return from South Africa, that "it was in Hardvar that I realized what a deep impression my humble services in South Africa had made throughout the whole of India" (ibid., p. 389).

In 1916 he demanded that the indenture system for immigration that the British had imposed on Indians be abolished. It consisted of a form of slavery whereby Indians who emigrated to British colonies were subjected to legal discrimination that treated them in a cruel manner, as if they were some kind of commercial chattel. Gandhi states:

> I felt, however, that India could not be satisfied with so very vague an assumption, but ought to agitate for immediate abolition. India had tolerated the system through her sheer negligence, and I believe the time had come when people could successfully agitate for redress ... It was time for me to tour the country for an all—India agitation. (Ibid., p. 400)

Gandhi started helping the poor who were mistreated and abused in South Africa and India. He also understood that when the *ryots'* (the name given to peasants) demands were aggressively crushed, "law courts were useless". He considered it necessary to teach the workers (peasants, etc.) not to be afraid of their employers by "making them realize that the officials were not the masters but the servants of the people ... *And ... to make them realize the duty of combining civility with fearlessness*" (ibid., p. 436, our emphasis). As the plague broke out in Rajkot, Gandhi volunteered his services and visited every locality, including the quarters of the untouchables, to inspect the latrines and teach the residents better methods of sanitation.

In 1919 when the British passed the so called "Rowlatt Act", which established that "certain political cases were to be tried without juries and permitted internment of suspects without trial", Gandhi called a general *hartal* on 6 April 1919, a twenty-four-hour general strike without violence, declared as a religious act for fasting and praying, that afterwards changed into civil disobedience. Seven days later in Punjab, what has been referred to as the "Jallianwala Bagh massacre" took place, where over a thousand Indians were killed or wounded on the orders of the British commander, Dyer. His troops fired at the crowd for ten minutes until they no longer had any ammunition. Such viciousness shocked the entire country, having an immediate impact on the people who started to become aware that, after all, the British were not really their protectors as they had believed until then. The anger further increased later, when the House of Lords honoured Dyer for his action, resulting in 1920 in the "Non Cooperation Movement".

Eleven years earlier, in 1909, Gandhi (1957) had stated that British rule was established in India with the cooperation of Indians and had remained until then because of that cooperation; if at any time they were to refuse this collaboration, the British would crumble and *swaraj*, meaning Indian self-rule, would take place. After the Jallianwala incident, Gandhi became determined to work intensively towards total independence of all Indian institutions and, at the beginning of 1921, he extended his non-cooperation into other forms of boycott, such as on British goods and educational institutions as well as in courts of law, resigning from government services, and relinquishing British titles and honours. Other violent clashes between both parties followed in Chauri Chaura and Uttar Pradesh, a situation that persuaded Gandhi, who was concerned about the violence, to resort to mass civil disobedience for a third time, leading to his arrest in March 1922, when he was charged with subversion and sentenced to six years' incarceration. However, two years later, due to acute appendicitis and the need for surgical intervention, he was released from jail.

In 1923 Gandhi stated that his desire was not only to free India from the British yoke, but also, and very importantly, to provide his country with economic and social freedom. He stayed out of main politics for several years, focusing only on the Indian National Congress and other issues of general interest, such as untouchability, alcoholism, ignorance, and poverty. In 1927 the British government produced a commission for the reform of the constitution that did not include Indians, a situation

that provoked strong reactions on several fronts, such as a boycott by
the Indian political parties and Gandhi's threat to achieve full independence in 1929. The lack of response from the British induced further
action, such as the unfurling of the Indian flag in 1930, the creation of
India's Independence Day by the Indian Congress, and the very significant Salt March against the salt tax in the same year, when Gandhi,
escorted by thousands of followers, marched 388 kilometres to the sea
in order to make salt himself. Britain reacted by incarcerating over
60,000 people. At the same time, the Indians reacted by making Gandhi
a national folk hero, a Messiah, and the Indian Congress made him its
sacred instrument. A pact was signed in 1931 between Gandhi and the
British, who released all political prisoners while Gandhi called for a
suspension of the civil disobedience movement. Also, he was invited
as the only representative of India to attend a round table conference in
London, which resulted in total disappointment because it only centred
on irrelevant matters and never discussed the issue of Indian independence. At the time, Winston Churchill, who was very critical of Gandhi
and often ridiculed him, had this to say:

> It is alarming and also nauseating to see Mr Gandhi, a seditious
> Middle Temple lawyer, now posing as a fakir of a type well known
> in the East, striding half-naked up the steps of the Vice-regal
> palace ... to parley on equal terms with the representative of the
> King-Emperor. (Herman, 2008, p. 359)

Whatever was achieved in the Gandhi-Irwin Pact in London, was completely destroyed by the new Viceroy, Lord Willingdon, even before
Gandhi had set foot in India. The country was being ruled by ordi-
nances, and shooting and arrests were then very common. Jawaharlal
Nehru, who was coming to Bombay to meet Gandhi, was arrested on
his way. After Gandhi landed on 28 December 1931, he said that those
were Christmas gifts from Lord Willingdon, "our Christian viceroy";
a week later he was also arrested.

When the Second World War started in 1939, Gandhi felt the need
to return to politics again. While addressing a session at the All India
Congress Committee on 7 August 1942, he said that his quarrel did not
come out of anger and was not against the British people, that he was
only fighting their imperialism. At the same time, the Indians disliked
the unilateral decision made by the British to include India in the war

without ever having consulted the people's representatives. As a consequence, all congressmen resigned from office and Gandhi announced publically that India would reject any participation in a war that "was fought by the English for democratic freedom, while India was denied of that freedom by the same people". Simultaneously, Gandhi and the Congress engaged in a continuous demand for independence, telling the British to leave India and demanding *Karo ya maro* ("Do or die") from their fellow citizens. The British responded with mass arrests and a level of violence never previously experienced.

In August 1942 Gandhi was arrested and held, along with members of the working committee, for two years. It was a very difficult time for Gandhi, since his wife Kasturba died after he had been in jail for a year and a half, and his secretary also died of a heart attack. Gandhi became very ill with malaria and was freed before serving his full sentence due to the fear of how his comrades would react if he had died in prison. India finally became independent from British domination on 15 August 1947. At the same time, Muslims were demanding partition and the creation of the state of Pakistan as an independent nation, something Gandhi opposed but had to accept in order to avoid civil war. Perhaps this separation, and his strong belief in non-violence, were the reasons for his assassination on 30 January 1948 in the garden of the former Birla House, as he was walking to pray at 5 pm accompanied by two of his grandnieces. He was shot three times in the chest, at point-blank range, by Nathuram Godse, a Hindu nationalist related to extremist Hindu Mahasabha, who felt Gandhi was guilty of favouring Pakistan and was strongly against violence. Some people believed that the same person, Nathuram Godse, had previously tried to kill Gandhi in 1934 and again ten years later in 1944; first with a bomb and the second time with a dagger.

Conclusion

We are trying to figure out the relationship between the phenomenology of Gandhi's pre-conceptual trauma and his capacity to accomplish the epic endeavour of liberating his country from a century of British domination, by means of non-violence and without ever shooting anybody. Non-violence or *ahimsa*, as Hindu Buddhists refers to it, stands for a form of "passive aggression" that contains two opposite dialectic attitudes or "false sub-selves", using Winnicott's contribution: an outward, "complying", or libidinal false self, and another "negativistic", hidden, or aggressive false self (López-Corvo, 2006a). "Complying" or "libidinal" is equal to *ahimsa*, and if acted out, will elicit opposite emotions such as negativism and aggression. Let us say for instance, that A, similar to Gandhi, presents a continuous complying attitude towards B; such interaction will unconsciously trigger, in B, the opposite emotion, meaning a negativistic or aggressive reaction. This is a dynamic often observed in what is referred to as "gender-based violence", between men and women. In this case, women being biologically less prone towards open aggression are usually more inclined to use libidinal, complying, or passive-aggressive behaviour, which automatically triggers open aggression in men, who will then appear as the sadistic perpetrator and the woman as the masochistic victim; sometimes, however, the roles can be inverted.

Gandhi, influenced by Tolstoy, intuitively resorted to non-violence to provoke the British, who due to their pride and culture, were more disposed to openly act out their frustration, as can be seen in what took place in the so-called "Jallianwala Bagh massacre", when, in April 1919, a week after Gandhi had called for a non-violent *hartal* or general strike, over a thousand Indians were murdered by the British government.

Being able to achieve what Gandhi did was the result of several factors. We prefer to discriminate between particulars, which were an immediate consequence of his own pre-conceptual trauma as it was structured during the first years of his life, and those general aspects resulting from his education and experience within Indian culture. However, it would be unreasonable to believe that Gandhi achieved what he did alone; there were many friends and political activists, often mentioned by him in his autobiography, who continuously contributed to his endeavour of achieving India's independence.

Reading his autobiography we can also observe in Gandhi a powerful need to feel important, significant (Gandhi, 1957, p. 202), as well as a need to take over and control almost everything he came close to, such as: forcing his wife to collect pots full of excrement from guests at his place, and, when she refused, threatening to kick her out even when she had nowhere to go (ibid., p. 277); being able to deliver his own children at birth, becoming their teacher at home (ibid., pp. 199–204); refusing to take medicine or to give them to his sick son, even when prescribed by a doctor, preferring instead to prescribe his own (ibid., 247); even washing his own clothes and cutting his own hair. He thought that something was true by the mere fact that he believed it, even if he did not have scientific proof. He read that milk would induce animal passions" (ibid., p. 328), and that abstinence from salt and pulses could stop a vaginal haemorrhage in his wife. He gave food an astounding level of importance, discriminating between those he would fanatically never touched because he felt they were extremely contaminating and dangerous, such as meat, milk, grains, or eggs, and those he considered particularly healthy, such as nuts and fruits. He also believed that sadomasochistic mechanisms were "true love"; for instance, he used victimisation and guilt in order to control his children's behaviour: if his children perpetrated any offence he would punish himself by fasting (ibid., pp. 342–343), with the excuse that it was his fault that they had reacted as they had.

Trying to control everything, as he did, could have several meanings, such as a form of identification with his mother, who was described as the ideal housewife, because she was "the first one to rise and the last to go to bed, eating only when she could manage it" (Erikson, 1969, p. 105); also, as a form of compensation for his feelings of insignificance resulting from being, as a child, the youngest in a very large family. In relation to this aspect we have previously described

> … a clinical condition present in some patients who have in common being the youngest child in their family, with an age difference from their immediate sibling of eight to ten years … The core of the conflict seems to hinge on the incongruence that a small child is able to induce in a family of adults, becoming, on the one hand, the centre of attention and on the other, someone absolutely irrelevant when important matters were at stake. Such inconsistency induces a severe splitting between a part I have referred to as the "significant" element and a correlated but opposite emotion I have also referred to as the "insignificant" one. (López-Corvo, 2014, p. 125)

Gandhi compensated to deal with his sense of insignificance; the need, for example, to act out a sense of "omnipotent significance" or unconsciously feeling that he was his mother's "narcissistic completion" (basic delusion),[3] or acting out the oedipal identification with his father and controlling everything he did, as if he were the only one who could do it "right". He used stubbornness in order to remain in control, feeling that he would always get his own way if he insisted. This could be a pattern resulting from overprotection, being the little one in a large family of adults. His phobia was a symptom, possibly a consequence of guilt and fear, produced by feelings of retaliation from the re-introjection of his oedipal desires of controlling his mother and taking his father's place. For instance, his desire to control and possess his mother could have produced fear of retaliation from his father and older siblings.

We can also consider several factors resulting from the environment and the circumstances he was exposed to during his adult life. There is his experience in South Africa, considered the place he learned most of the strategies he later applied in his own country. In South Africa, similar to other immigrants, he was mistreated, something that unconsciously could have made him feel that he "did not deserve his mother's love", but he was very stubborn and the more he was rejected, the more effort he made. In the end, he became all Hindus. There was also the family tradition of occupying important political positions.

CHAPTER EIGHTEEN

Picasso

Is not very common to find someone with as many names as Picasso had. He was baptised Pablo Diego José Francisco de Paula Juan Nepomuceno María de los Remedios Cipriano de la Santísima Trinidad y Picasso. In the end he chose to use only the first and last names, because he felt the others, with the exception of Picasso, his mother's family name of Italian extraction and unusual in his language, were too common in Spanish. He was born in 1881 as the eldest child of José Ruiz y Blasco (1838–1913) and María Picasso y López (1855–1939), into a middle-class family from Malaga in Andalucía, at the southern tip of Spain.

Jose Ruiz, Picasso's father, was an art teacher who specialised in painting birds, and unlike his brothers, who were successful in their professions, José had financial difficulties most of his life. At the age of thirty-eight he was still living with his parents, overprotected by his sisters, regularly visiting local brothels, and a confirmed bachelor. He was nicknamed the "Englishman" due to his charm, manners, and good looks. Picasso, the son, often complained of not having inherited the "aristocratic" appearance of his father.

Although José exhibited the inclination and the sensitivity of an artist, he lacked the outstanding gift and temperament later displayed by his son; however, Picasso's grandfather, Diego Ruiz, a businessman by profession, was very enthusiastic about the arts, drew, and played the contrabass in the local orchestra; he also registered his two older sons, José and Pablo, in an art institute in Malaga, and it is possible that José's interest in painting originated from this time. Pablo, Picasso's uncle, later became a doctor in theology and a canon at Malaga cathedral, but he always maintained his interest in art. Salvador, the youngest of the children, married the daughter of a well-known sculptor who considered himself a "lover of all the arts". With all these significant artistic leanings in the family, it is unsurprising that Pablo Picasso was influenced to become a painter.

Pressured by his family after his father Diego's death, José, Picasso's father, decided to get married, although not to the candidate his family had chosen, but with María Picasso López, his cousin. Around this time, José had to face two difficult financial constraints; the family vineyard was ruined by a disease, and Pablo, his oldest brother who had financially supported him all of his life and in whose house he had always lived, died. However, a sad event that happened at this time came to José's rescue; Salvador, the youngest and wealthiest of all of them, who lived in a large house, lost his wife and in order to get help to raise his children, asked his sisters to come and live with him, as well as uncle José. At the same time, Salvador used his influence in the field of art and found a job for José as a curator in the Malaga municipal museum and as a teacher in the School of Fine Art.

Francisco Picasso Guardeño, María Picasso's father and Picasso's maternal grandfather, was the fifth child of Tomas Picasso and Maria Guardeño. In his youth he studied in England, something unusual for the Spanish middle class of the time. He had six daughters in a common law relationship with Inés López Robles (1831–1902), the daughter of a barrel maker; however, they got married sometime later, in 1864, as their wedding was delayed possibly because his family was opposed to it, as she had a lower social background. He abandoned Inés, María Picasso's mother, and her five sisters and went to live and work in Cuba for the next fifteen years, although he was able to look after them by regularly sending money. However, when he finally decided to return, the boat he boarded in Havana stopped in Matanzas (Cuba) where he got yellow fever and died (Sabartés, 1954).

José Ruiz Blasco and María Picasso y López, Picasso's parents, married a year after his brother Pablo's death; she was seventeen years younger than him, optimistic, lively and with a subtle sense of humour. María Picasso and her five sisters grew up without a man in her family, and she hardly knew her father. When she became pregnant with Picasso, she prayed to have a son as her first baby, and when he was born, they named him Pablo like his uncle, and the whole family partied as if "the Messiah had arrived". Two girls were born afterwards, Maria Dolores (Lola) and Maria Concepción (Conchita). Picasso, the only boy in two generations, grew up in Andalucía under the special care of his mother who adored him, his maternal grandmother Ines López Robles, as well as two aunts, Eladia and Heliodora. They became, in his memory, "a warm and kind reminiscence from this time of his life". For seven years he was the only child until his sister Dolores birth in 1887, and grew up as the only boy surrounded by women.

Picasso was a child prodigy and, according to his mother, the first word he spoke as a child was "*piz*", short for "*lápiz*", pencil in Spanish, that he requested to scribble with, and, imitating his father, to draw spirals, before he was fully able to talk. From the age of seven, he began receiving formal training from his father, and at the age of eight painted his first oil painting. He detested school, disliking anything that had to do with numbers with the same intensity that he loved art. It is said that he could have suffered from some kind of dyslexia as a child, because he confused numbers, as he privileged shape over value and saw in the number seven an upside down house and a woman kneeling in the number two.

At the end of 1890 the family moved to La Coruña in search of a better living, leaving behind in Malaga the grandmother Inés and the two maternal aunts. Thanks again to his brother Salvador's connections, José managed to secure a position as a teacher in the institute of art in La Coruña. The move represented a difficult change for all of them, and several years later, during an interview when he reminisced about those times, Picasso said: "my father had suffered similar to Napoleon when transferred to the island of St. Elena … [he had] no Malaga, no bullfighting, nor friends, nothing" (Richardson, 1991, p. 34). La Coruña, the main port in Galicia, located at the northeast extreme of the Iberian Peninsula, has inclement weather, particular if you are from a warmer climate such as that in the south of Spain. Also, life there for the Ruiz family was not free from financial difficulties. All of these limitations had a negative influence on José, who became rather taciturn and depressed, refusing to go out or to attend bullfighting, and so on. His son Pablo, on the other hand, took great pleasure in this new home, to the point that he learned the local dialect and recited and sang in Gallego. Possibly he was enjoying his new freedom, away from his grandmother, aunts, and uncles who out of too much concern restricted his autonomy. He did poorly at the elementary school and according to his own testimony, "I was a poor student, and they used to punishment me … It was my way to be by myself, not to be bothered and to be able to draw and draw and draw …" (ibid., p. 42). According to Picasso, hard work as well as energy and concentration came naturally to him because it was inherited from his mother. Perhaps, as we might insist further on, this capacity to produce was a consequence of his oedipal competition towards his depressed and limited father.

In 1895 Conchita died of diphtheria at the age of seven, a tragedy that came as such a blow to the whole family that they decided to move to Barcelona. Picasso, aged fourteen, was also very affected by his sister's death, and forty years later, in 1935, gave his first daughter, better known as Maya, the same name. His father became so depressed that at one point he felt unable to finish a picture of pigeons, because he was having difficulty drawing their claws and asked Picasso if he could finish it for him. When sometime later he came to examine the painting, he was immensely impressed with Picasso's ability to draw, to the extent that he decided, recognising his son's prodigy, to pass his brushes, oil paints, and palette on to him. In 1950, when contemplating his work "Still life with pigeons", Picasso exclaimed: "I had paid my father with pigeons" (ibid., p. 52). As an adolescent Picasso painted, as a master, anything he attempted, such as landscapes, portraits, mythological figures, animals, and so on; his work was so well done that he was not allowed to participate in children's exhibitions. After they moved to Barcelona, Picasso who was then fourteen years old, turned into a more serious student, and a year later he was admitted to advanced classes in the Royal Academy of Art in Barcelona, where he passed the admission exam, which usually required weeks of preparation, in just one day, impressing the teachers who gave him the highest marks.

When he turned sixteen he was sent to Madrid and registered at the Royal Academy of San Fernando; however, he became bored and disillusioned with the work at the academy, because the rigidity and emphasis placed on classical work restricted his freedom and his own creativity. He preferred to spend his time visiting museums in order to admire the work of masters such as Velazquez and Zurbarán. The academy then advised his father to stop sending him money. Later on, in 1901, together with his anarchist friend Francisco de Asis Soler he created the magazine *Arte Joven*, in which he produced political cartoons and Francisco did the writing. It was the first time that he signed himself as "Picasso". He travelled to Paris for the first time in 1900, and later, in 1904, at the age of twenty-three, he settled there permanently, making a few short visits to Spain before the outbreak of the Civil War. He remained in Paris even after the Nazi occupation, although it was forbidden for his work to be exhibited. Finally he moved to the south of France where he remained until his death in April of 1973.

It has been calculated that by the time of his death, Picasso had created the amazing total of around 22.000 works of art, in a diversity of forms, such as painting, drawing, sculpture, ceramics, mosaic, and graphic art. Due to this immense productivity his work has been classified into different periods according to the time of their creation: the Blue, from 1901 to 1904, the Rose from 1905 to 1907, the African from 1908 to 1909, the Analytic Cubism from 1909 to 1912 and the Synthetic Cubism from 1912 to 1919.

A very important friend from this time was the Catalan artist Carles Casagemas (1881–1901), who became a regular companion during the time he lived in Barcelona and who accompanied Picasso during his first trip to Paris in 1900. A year older than Picasso, Casagemas was emotionally unstable, self-destructive, and addicted to alcohol and narcotics. A year later, on 17 February 1901, Casagemas shot himself after attempting to kill his girlfriend Germaine Gargallo (1880–1948) at a dinner celebration with Catalan expatriates at L'Hippodrome Café in Paris. Apparently, Germaine had rejected Casagemas' proposal of marriage, possibly because he was sexually impotent. His suicide had a significant emotional impact on Picasso, and, according to some art critics, determined his "Blue Period" where he expressed his concern with mortality and human suffering, producing at least three paintings dedicated to Casagemas' suicide: "Casagemas in his Coffin", "Evocation (The Burial of Casagemas)", and "*La Vie*" (The Life).

"*La Vie*" is a very symbolic and interesting picture painted in May 1903, approximately three months after Casagemas' death, which portrays a great deal, not only about him, but also about Picasso's unconscious. To the front and on the left side, a naked couple are standing; the woman, maybe representing Germaine, is leaning on the man, with an empty gaze as if lost in her own concerns. The man, who resembles

Casagemas, is wearing underwear, indicating a physical separation from the naked woman, maybe symbolic of Casagemas' sexual impotence. He is also vaguely exchanging looks and clearly, but secretly, pointing with his left hand to a woman standing on the right side of the picture who is dressed and holding a little child in her arms. She has a serious and hard countenance, looking straight at Casagemas and giving the impression that she is reproaching him for something, as if they are emotionally related, that possibly she is his mother.

As was customary at the time, Casagemas was a regular user of narcotics and alcohol, and we know from experience that addictions are always proportionally related to the absence of the father and to a strong presence of the mother. On the other hand, sexual impotence, of psychological cause, can be unconsciously linked to unresolved oedipal dependency on the mother, meaning that if he is unconsciously looking for his mother in every woman, sex with them could be experienced as a form of incest that would automatically result in impotence. In the background of the picture is a seated naked couple, where a woman seems to be holding and consoling a man in distress. In the background also but below the couple, there is a naked man, alone, with his head between his legs and his eyes closed, looking depressed and destitute. These images speak of Picasso's amazing intuitive ability to grasp his friend's emotional conflict and to be able to reproduce them with such outstanding precision. There is also the possibility that the sudden death of his friend could have triggered memories from the past, from the time Picasso's little sister Conchita died, representing a form of what Freud (1896) referred to as *nachträglichkeit* or "deferred action", and Lacan (1953) as *après coup*; meaning that traumas in the present will always trigger pre-conceptual traumas or traumas from the past (López-Corvo, 2014). We have already referred to this matter in Chapter One as "trauma entanglement".

After Casagemas' death, Picasso became Germaine's lover, a situation that might have induced guilt in him, as he might have felt that it was convenient for him that his friend had disappeared; a state of affairs possibly similar to which he could have experienced as a child when, after his youngest sister's death, he regained his mother's attention. Death of younger siblings always produces ambivalent feelings, as children normally love and hate each other since they feel that they have been "left out" because another sibling has been chosen, something that produces envy and the desire for the other sibling to disappear or to die, and because children use omnipotent feelings or magic belief, they think that they can kill just by thinking; when this happens, as in the case of Conchita, this induces strong feelings of guilt and a need for punishment. Picasso named his first daughter, also known as Maya, Maria Concepción, like his deceased sister.

There is another picture from the same Blue Period titled "The Tragedy", which portrays three dressed figures: a man, a woman, and a boy standing barefoot by the seashore with the sky and an empty sea as the background. The man has a beard—like Picasso's father—and is looking down with an expression of concern, shame, and resignation; his arms are crossed in front, with his hands hidden, giving the impression of either being cold or feeling helpless, while his left leg, bent a little, seems to stress a sense of shame and helplessness. The boy is next to the old man with his right hand open and touching the old man slightly, as if he is reassuring or consoling him, while the gesture made with his left hand, together with a rather concerned and sad gaze looking beyond, gives the impression of either providing an explanation to the couple or trying to solve a dilemma of his own, or both. The woman seems distant, looking down at the boy with pouting lips, as if furtively throwing him a kiss.

An important aspect of this picture is its title; why did Picasso name it "The Tragedy"? Where is the tragedy in this picture? We believe this painting portrays Picasso's parents and himself as an adolescent and possibly represents the conflictual mental dilemma all adolescents have to face when breaking away from their family in order to find their own identity, their freedom, and their own place in life. It is a concern that Picasso, being such a gifted child, could have intra-psychically experienced earlier than the point at which he decided, while living in Madrid, not to attend the Academy of Art, as his father wished, but to wander around different museums to observe the work of the great masters. Or, when back in Barcelona, he joined the Bohemian group of artists at the "Els Quatre Gats" (The Four Cats) coffee shop, and his family complained about the kind of life he was leading. Or when he finally left for Paris in 1901, where he stayed until the end of his life, although sporadically taking short visits to Spain. Strong will and determination were important features in Picasso's idiosyncrasy.

There are important aspects in Picasso's oedipal dynamics that we would like to summarise. First, there is the great importance his mother bestowed on the birth of a boy—Picasso being the first in two generations—as she grew up fatherless in a family of seven women, her mother and five sisters. Her fear of losing him as an infant was so great, something common in those times, that she resorted to providing him with an unusual rosary of names, from saints and dead relatives, possibly so as to have various entities protecting him from "above". But his mother was not the only woman living in Picasso's home; there was his maternal grandmother and also two aunts from his mother's side, who, similar to Maria Picasso, had experienced the absence of men. In the early years of his life, during the time when human character is definitely structured, Picasso was surrounded and raised by four women who adored and spoiled him. To this situation we have to add the fact that he was not an ordinary child; this was a home where art and crafts were idealised and Picasso was already painting like Rembrandt when he was still a child. The other aspect to consider, perhaps even more significantly, was the fact that his father, who was an artist and a teacher of art, recognised, when Picasso was only fourteen years old, that he was indeed much more gifted than himself and decided to pass on to him his palette and oil paints, which was an uncommon attitude between a father and such a young son sharing the same trade. Was this the lesser, shamed, and destitute father that Picasso painted in "The Tragedy"? Is he the father that he is trying to console and reassure in the picture? And does the mother, throwing a kiss from a distance, represent a form of secret love, of a mother saying to the child, "I think more highly of you than I do of your father"? After all, José Ruiz Blasco was a depressed, limited, and poor provider who constantly required help from his brother Salvador.

There are at least three main features that stand out in Picasso's adult character: his industrious creativity, strong personality, and being an incorrigible "Don Juan". His industrious creativity could be the consequence of a powerful and ambitious need to achieve, possibly in competition with his father in order to obtain his mother's recognition and love, among many other factors; his strong and determined personality could be the result of the attention and worship bestowed by all the women who surrounded him as a child. Finally, his ambivalence of love and hate, or perhaps better, of need and rejection, towards women, who he once referred to as "goddesses or doormats" (Venning, 2012); goddesses, perhaps, when he needed them and doormats once he rejected them. When he rejected them he felt guilty and, in order to make amends, he did anything to seduce them, but, sometime later, this need angered him so he rejected them, and so on. One of his mistresses, Argentinean born Dora Maar, once said of him: "As an artist you may be extraordinary, but morally speaking you are worthless." Picasso married twice, first in 1917 to Olga Stepanovna Khokhlova (1891–1955), a ballerina from the Ukraine who died of cancer in 1955 and with whom he had a boy named Paolo. His second marriage was in 1961 with Jacqueline Roque (1927–986), who he met in 1953 when he was seventy-two and she twenty-seven years old, after drawing the picture of a dove on the wall of her house and bringing a flower every day until she agreed to date him; they were married for eleven years until his death on 8 April 1973, in Mougins, France. Besides these marriages, Picasso was often involved in affairs with several other women, often with two or three at the same time, who provided great inspiration for his work, although in some cases at a great cost, since two of them became mentally ill and two others committed suicide. Among them were: Fernande Olivier, Eva Gouell, Marie-Thérèse Walter, Dora Maar, Françoise Gilot, Genevieve Laporte, and Jacqueline Roque. He had four children, one boy, Paul, with Olga Kakhlova, his first wife, one girl, Maya (Maria Conchita), with Marie-Thérèse, and two children, Claude and Paloma, with Francoise Gilot.

CHAPTER NINETEEN

General consideration

T his book is the product of an investigation consisting of the comparison of two different groups of individuals chosen at random, although based on the existence of well-documented biographies. One group consists of five well-known dictators who ruled their countries with iron fists for several years; the other group represents five, also well-known, individuals, internationally recognised for their outstanding creativity. The comparison was established using a theoretical model we have documented in great detail in Chapter One.

In summary we have considered that the personality or character structure of every human being is mostly established by the complex combination of genetic determinants, cultural influences, and traumatic circumstances. We have only regarded in this investigation the particular traumatic events that take place during the first years of life, which we refer to as "pre-conceptual traumas". We have defined a situation as traumatic when a temporary absence changes into a permanent presence that unconsciously will repeat forever. We will clarify with a vignette:

> A mother once consulted me feeling very concerned about her three-year-old boy's new habit of spitting everywhere and at everybody. I asked her if she wished for this behaviour to disappear or to

become permanent. "Well no, to disappear," she answered. Then I said: "If you can contain this behaviour and say nothing it will extinguish itself in a few days, but if you get into a power struggle to see who will overcome who, it might contain you both, and although it might disappear after a while, it might come back subsequently, either in the same manner or transformed into a metaphor, and he might not remember why" (López-Corvo, 2014, p. XXVIII).

There are two forms of traumas, "pre-conceptual" and "conceptual", the former ubiquitous and the latter accidental. Pre-conceptual traumas represent "preconceptions" that have taken place during the first years of life, when there is not a mind capable of containing and endowing them with a sensible meaning, different from "conceptual traumas", which occur at a later age, at a time when there is a mind already, which fails to contain the traumatic facts; there is extensive literature about this later form of trauma. Pre-conceptual traumas are the product—among many other factors—of the discrepancy between the helplessness of the child and the ascendancy of the parents who are just ordinary people. Pre-conceptual traumas always split the mind in two opposite states which continuously and dialectically interact: "the traumatised" and the "non-traumatised state"; the traumatised state results from the compulsive repetition of the pre-conceptual traumas. It will organise the mind of an individual and will define his or her idiosyncrasy, occupation, choice of partners, ways of life, form of suffering or not, and so on. The non-traumatised on the other hand, represents the mental development that will normally take place from birth to adulthood.[1]

We have studied the first years of life of the individuals we have investigated and then compared the two groups in order to find similarities and differences between them. We have found great similarities between the individuals within each group, but great disparities in the comparison of the two groups. We first try to summarise the most common characteristics we have found within each group and then try to establish a comparison between them. All the subjects we have evaluated are males, because this was the gender historically found in totalitarian regimes, and in order to match this group with creative persons we were forced to choose male individuals. We have produced a comparative table showing the most important variables present in all the subjects.

NOTES

Introduction

1. An illegitimate patient I have had for some time in analyses proudly expressed that he was father to twenty-five illegitimate children.

Chapter One

1. Heraclitus (540-480 BCE), a poet and philosopher from Ephesus, believed in the concept of a "perpetual change" in all things, and that the only abiding permanent feature of reality was the Logos (Λογοσ), or orderly principle, according to which all change takes place. He once stated that "no man can ever step in the same river twice".
2. A term Bion has borrowed from Poincaré, representing an emotional experience capable of providing order and coherence to a complexity of elements that up to that moment have been scattered and seemingly unrelated (Bion, 1962, p. 87).
3. A concept borrowed by Bion from Hume to explain how some mental facts that have been associated by chance remain conjoined and repeat by causality.

Chapter Three

1. By making this statement we are in no way accusing Che Guevara of being a coward. What we are trying to express is that men in general, being exposed to life-threatening situations, such as war, have to deal in their minds with feelings of castration anxiety that will enhance any realistic fears of being killed, and, at the same time, feelings that compensate, such as the need to prove themselves brave, usually by means of suicide. When these actions are successful, they produce dead, or, if they are lucky, alive well-decorated heroes.

Chapter Four

1. An estimated thirty-five to fifty serial killers are operating in the United States at any given time, and about a dozen are arrested each year, retired FBI agent John Douglas wrote on his website: www. johndouglasmindhunter.com.

Chapter Six

1. Original poem in Spanish:
   "No he de callar, por más que con el dedo,
   ya tocando la boca, o ya la frente,
   silencio avises, o amenaces miedo
   ¿No ha de haber un espíritu valiente?
   ¿Siempre se ha de sentir lo que se siente?
   ¿Nunca se ha de decir lo que se siente?"
2. There is a pun made with Fidel Castro's name, because in Spanish, "Fidel" means "loyal", "faithful".

Chapter Seven

1. In Spanish, the sense of mental pain, disillusionment, despair, and depression experienced when the loved one deceives or deserts her/his lover, is colloquially known as *despecho* (Italian = *dispetto*), a composed word formed by *"des"* meaning "without", and *"pecho"*, meaning "breast"; in other words, "breastless".
2. "Individual" is a word of Latin origin meaning "undivided".

Chapter Eleven

1. A form of agonising torture where the arms of a person are dislocated by pulling them upwards from behind, while at the same time pushing the head downwards.

Chapter Fourteen

1. All quotes from Solomon have been taken from his book in Spanish: *Beethoven, Biografía e Historia*, 1983.

Chapter Seventeen

1. See Chapter Eight.
2. This troubled relationship between Harilal and his father is the subject of a film produced in 2007—*Gandhi, My Father*.
3. See Chapter Eight.

Chapter Nineteen

1. There is an internet short story that we feel could be relevant to what we are now trying to explain:

> One evening an old Cherokee told his grandson about a battle that goes on inside people. He said, "My son, the battle is between two wolves inside us all. One is Evil—it is anger, envy, jealousy, sorrow, regret, greed, arrogance, self-pity, guilt, resentment, inferiority, lies, false pride, superiority, and ego. The other is Good—it is joy, peace, love, hope, serenity, humility, kindness, benevolence, empathy, generosity, truth, compassion, and faith." The grandson thought about it for a minute and then asked his grandfather: "Which wolf wins?" The old Cherokee simply replied, "The one you feed".

REFERENCES

Adroer, S. (1996). Fixation of asthma and sexual impotence at different stages. *International Journal of Psycho-analysis, 77*: 782–806.

Anderson, J. L. (1997). *Che*. New York: Grove Press.

Bergson, H. (1911). *Creative Evolution*. New York: Henry Holt & Company.

Bion, W. R. (1948). *Experience in Groups*. London: Tavistock, 1961.

Bion, W. R. (1962). *Learning from Experience*. London: Karnac, 1984.

Bion, W. R. (1965). Transformations. In: *Seven Servants*. London: Karnac.

Bion, W. R. (1967). *Second Thoughts: Selected Papers on Psycho-Analysis*. London: Karnac, 1993.

Bion, W. R. (1970). *Attention and Interpretation*. London: Karnac, 1984.

Brackman, R. (2001). *The Secret File of Joseph Stalin: A Hidden Life*. London: Frank Cass.

Chang, J., & Halliday, J. (2005). *Mao: The Unknown Story*. New York: Alfred A. Knopf.

Chomsky, N. (1989). *Necessary Illusions: Thought Control in Democratic Societies*. Boston: South End Press.

Edwards, J. (1993). *Persona Non Grata: A Memoir of Disenchantment with the Cuban Revolution*. New York: Nation Books.

Einstein, A. (1954). *Ideas and Opinions*. New York: Crown.

Erikson, E. H. (1969). *Gandhi's Truth: On the Origins of Militant Nonviolence*. New York: W.W. Norton, 1993.

Esteban, A., & Panichelli, S. (2004). *Gabo y Fidel, El Paisaje de una Amistad.* Madrid: Espasa-Calpe.

Freud, S. (1896). The aetiology of hysteria. *S. E., 3*: 189–224. London: Hogarth.

Freud, S. (1916d). Some character types met with in psycho-analytic work. *S. E., 14*: 309–332. London: Hogarth.

Freud, S. (1925). An autobiographical study. *Internet: http://www.mhweb.org/mpc_course/freud.pdf.*

Gandhi, M. K. (1957). *An Autobiography: The Story of my Experiment with Truth.* Boston: Beacon Press. (First published in serial form in 1927.)

Gandhi, M. K. (1958–1994). (CWMG): *The Collected Works of Mahatma Gandhi* (Electronic Book), New Delhi, Publications Division of the Government of India, Navajivan, 1999, 98 volumes. (Henceforth, CWM G).

Gandhi, M. K. (1964). *The Law of Continence: Brahmacharya.* Bombay: Bharatiya Vidya Bhavan.

García Marquez, G. (2006). El Fidel Castro que yo conozco. Granma Internacional, Noticias, August 4th. *Internet: http://www.diariocolatino.com/gabriel-garcia-marquez-el-fidel-castro-que-yo-conozco-2/.*

Gay, P. (1988). *Freud: A Life of Our Time.* New York: W. W. Norton.

Girzone, J. F. (1989). Saint Francis of Assisi. Foreword. In: G. K. Chesteron, *Saint Francis of Assisi.* Toronto: Doubleday.

Grotstein, J. (2004). The seventh servant: The implications of a truth drive in Bion's theory of "O." *International Journal of Psycho-Analysis, 85*: 1081–1101.

Herman, A. (2008). *Gandhi & Churchill: The Epic Rivalry that Destroyed an Empire and Forged Our Age.* London: Random House.

Hoffmann, B. (1972). *Albert Einstein: Creator & Rebel.* New York: Plume.

Jones, E. (1961). *The Life and Work of Sigmund Freud.* New York: Basic.

Khan, M. R. (1963). The Concept of Cumulative Trauma. *Psychoanalytic Study of the Child, 18*: 286–306.

Klein, M. (1952). Some theoretical conclusions regarding the emotional life of the infant. In: *Envy and Gratitude and Other Works.* London: Hogarth, 1975.

Kolakowski, L. (1985). *Main Currents of Marxism: The Founders, The Golden Age, The Breakdown.* New York: W. W. Norton.

Kubizek, A. (1976). *The Young Hitler I Knew.* Westport, CT: Greenwood.

Lacan, J. (1953). The function and field of speech and language in psychoanalysis. In: *Écrits: A Selection* (trans. A, Sheridan). London: Tavistock, 1977.

Langer, W. C. (1972). *The Mind of Adolf Hitler: The Secret Wartime Report.* New York: Basic.

López-Corvo, R. E. (1993). A Kleinian understanding of addiction. *Melanie Klein and Object Relations Journal, 11*: 1 June 1993.

López-Corvo, R. E. (2003). *The Dictionary of the Work of W. R. Bion*. London: Karnac.

López-Corvo, R. E. (2006a). Forgotten self, with the use of Bion's theory of negative links. *Psychoanalytic Review, 93*: 363–377.

López-Corvo, R. E. (2006b). *Wild Thoughts Searching for a Thinker: A Clinical Application of W. R. Bion's Theories*. London: Karnac.

López-Corvo, R. E. (2009). *The Women Within*. London: Karnac.

López-Corvo, R. E. (2012). Plato's theory of "form" and homeomorphic transformation of pre-conceptual traumas using Bion's model of container–contained. *Psychoanalytic Review, 99*.

López-Corvo, R. E. (2013). The distortion between "conceptual" and "preconceptual" traumas. *Psychoanalytic Review, 100*.

López-Corvo, R. E. (2014) *Traumatised and Non-traumatised States of the Personality: A Clinical Understanding Using Bion's Approach*. London: Karnac.

Marx, K. (1848). *Manifesto of the Communist Party*. London: Penguin, 1998.

Marx, K. (1861). *Internet: https://www.marxists.org/archive/marx/works/1861/ letter*.

Masson, J. L. (1974). India and the Unconscious: Erik Erikson on Gandhi. *International Journal of Psycho-Analysis, 55*: 519–526.

Meltzer, D. (1992). *The Claustrum: An Investigation of Claustrophobic Phenomena*. London: Clunie Press.

Miller, A. (1990). *For Your Own Good*. New York: Noonday Press.

Montefiore, S. S. (2003). *Stalin: The Court of the Red Tsar*. New York: Vintage.

Myerson, D. (2000). *Blood and Splendour*. New York: Perennial.

Neruda, P. (1954). *Las uvas y el viento*. Barcelona: Seix Barral, 1976.

Popper, K. R. (1971). *The Open Society and its Enemies*, Vol II. Princeton: Princeton University Press.

Press Trust of India. (2014). *Internet: http://indianexpress.com/article/india/ india-others/mahatmas-letter-accusing-son-of-rape-up-for-auction-in-uk/*.

Racker, H. (1948). Sobre un caso de impotencia, asma y conducta masoquista. *Revista. Psicoanalítica, 21*: 293–357.

Radosh, R. (2005). FrontPageMag.com, *18 October*.

Raffy, S. (2004). *Castro el Desleal*. : Santillana Ediciones.

Rauschning, H. (1940). *The Voice of Destruction: Conversations with Hitler*, 1940 New York: G. P Putman's Sons.

Richardson, J. (1991). *A Life of Picasso: Volume 1*. New York: Random House.

Sabartés, J. (1954). *Picasso. Documents iconographiques*. Ginebra.

Šebek, M. (1996). The Fate of the Totalitarian Object. *International Forum of Psycho-Analysis, 5*: 289–294.

Service, R. (2004). *Stalin: A Biography*. London: Pan.

Solomon, M. (1977). *Beethoven*. New York: Schirmer.

Tellenbach, M. E. (1983). *Beethoven and his "Immortal Beloved" Josephine Brunsvik: Her Fate and the Influence on Beethoven's Oeuvre*. Zurich: Atlantis.

Vargas Llosa, A. (2012). The Killing Machine, Che Guevara, from Communist Firebrand to Capitalist Brand. Internet: *The New Republic:* http://www.independent.org/newsroom/article.asp?id=1535.

Venning, A. (2012). How Picasso who called all women goddesses or doormats drove his lovers to despair. *Mail Online, 7 March 2012. http://www.dailymail.co.uk/femail/article-2111329/How-Picasso-called-women-goddesses-doormats-drove-lovers-despair-suicide-cruelty-betrayal.html.*

Victor, G. (1998). *Hitler: The Pathology of Evil*. Washington: Brassey.

Volkogonov, D. (1990). *Triumph and Tragedy*. New York: Grove Press.

Weber, T. (2004). *Gandhi as Disciple and Mentor*. Cambridge: University Press.

Winnicott, D. W. (1960). Ego distortion in terms of true and false self. In: *The Maturational Processes and the Facilitating Environment* (pp. 140–152). New York: International Universities Press.

Wolin, R. (1992). *The Heidegger Controversy*. Cambridge, MA: MIT Press.

INDEX